Project-Oriented Leadership

Project-Oriented Leadership

RALF MÜLLER and J RODNEY TURNER

GOWER

Published by
Gower Publishing Limited
Wey Court East
Union Road
Farnham
Surrey, GU9 7PT
England

Gower Publishing Company
Suite 420
101 Cherry Street
Burlington
VT 05401-4405
USA

www.gowerpublishing.com

Ralf Müller and J Rodney Turner have asserted their moral right under the Copyright, Designs and Patents Act, 1988, to be identified as the authors of this work.

British Library Cataloguing in Publication Data
Muller, Ralf, 1957-
  Project-oriented leadership. -- (Advances in project management)
  1. Project management. 2. Leadership.
  I. Title II. Series III. Turner, J. Rodney (John Rodney), 1953-
  658.4'04-dc22

  ISBN: 978-0-566-08923-7 (hbk)
        978-1-4094-0939-7 (ebk)

Library of Congress Cataloging-in-Publication Data
M|ller, Ralf, 1957-
  Project-oriented leadership / by Ralf M|ller and J. Rodney Turner.
    p. cm. -- (Advances in project management)
  Includes bibliographical references and index.
  ISBN 978-0-566-08923-7 (hardback) -- ISBN 978-1-4094-0939-7 (ebook)
  1. Project management. 2. Leadership. I. Turner, J. Rodney (John Rodney), 1953- II. Title.
  HD69.P75M856 2010
  658.4'092--dc22

                                                                    2010010162

Printed and bound in Great Britain by
MPG Books Group, UK

CONTENTS

LIST OF FIGURES

LIST OF TABLES

CHAPTER 1

INTRODUCTION

TWO BELIEFS

In the project management community, there are two pervading beliefs. At first sight these two beliefs appear to be different, because one ignores the project manager and the other focuses on the project manager. But as we shall see, they are two sides of the same coin.

The first belief is that project management is all about tools and techniques. Anybody who learns the tools and techniques can manage a project. Over the years, many lists of success factors have been produced. The most famous by Jeffrey Pinto and Dennis Slevin (1987) is shown in Table 1.1.

Table 1.1   List of success factors due to Pinto and Slevin (1987)

Success factor	Description
1. Project mission	Clearly defined goals and direction
2. Top management support	Resources, authority and power for implementation
3. Schedule and plans	Detailed specification of implementation process
4. Client consultation	Communication with and consultation of all stakeholders
5. Personnel	Recruitment, selection and training of competent personnel
6. Technical tasks	Ability of the required technology and expertise
7. Client acceptance	Selling of the final product to the end users
8. Monitoring and feed back	Timely and comprehensive control
9. Communication	Provision of timely data to key players
10. Trouble-shooting	Ability to handle unexpected problems

This lists ten success factors of projects, but makes no mention of the project manager. In gathering their data, they asked project managers to say what they thought success factors were on their projects, and perhaps they were all too modest to mention themselves. You might also say that the project manager's competence is implied by many of the items in the list. The project manager needs to be competent at planning, at communicating with the customer, at trouble shooting. But still, no direct mention is made of the project manager, and his or her competence, including traits and behaviours, and particularly leadership style. This is common with many of the similar lists produced, (Turner and Müller

2005, 2006). An extreme example was an advertisement for a software product in a British project management magazine that said, 'If you can move a mouse you can manage a project.' Buy our software product; that is all you need to manage a project. You don't need to be competent at project management, and you don't need appropriate traits and behaviours, and you don't need to lead the project team. Rodney's daughter aged three could move a mouse, so a three-year-old can be a project manager.

The second belief says that once you have learnt the tools and techniques, you can apply them to any project, regardless of your domain knowledge, your traits and behaviours, your temperament and your leadership style. You can go from managing a computer project to an organizsational change project to the construction of a nuclear power station. All you need is your kit bag of project management tools and techniques. Rodney examined a PhD once where the candidate had investigated six organizational change projects in six different companies. One of the projects was in a large engineering construction company. To manage the project, the company had chosen its two best project managers from the field, two men who were very effective at bullying subcontractors to deliver on time and cost. They were not successful at managing the internal change project, where you must motivate stakeholders to support the change and communicate well with them. The two men who were extremely effective project managers in the field did not have the appropriate temperament for managing organizational change.

These two beliefs are two sides of the same coin. One ignores the project manager, while the other says a project manager can manage any project. But they both imply that project management is all about mastering the tools and techniques. The project manager's competence does not contribute to project success. Yes the project manager must be competent at applying the tools. But competence is more than just skills at using tools; it also comprises appropriate traits and behaviours, including effective leadership style.

MANAGERS AND LEADERS

In this book we aim to show that successful project management is more than just the effective application of tools and techniques. Successful project management also depends on the leadership competence and the management competence of the project manager. Leadership and management are terms often used interchangeably. There are, however, significant differences between the two. Bennis and Nanus (1985) define the difference as:

> *To manage means to bring about, to accomplish, to have responsibility for, to conduct. Leading is influencing, guiding in direction, course, action, and*

opinion. This distinction is crucial. Managers are people who do things right and leaders are people who do the right things.

Both management and leadership competences are needed for sustainable success in a management position. A manager (or leader) showing only strengths in one of the two competence areas will find it difficult to maintain a high-performing team in the long run. In a recent interview in *Director*, the magazine of the UK's Institute of Directors, Henry Mintzberg said the separation of management and leadership is dysfunctional: leaders who don't manage won't know what is going on; management without leadership is demoralizing. Ken Parry (2004) summarizes this in Table 1.2. This shows that that people with good managerial but poor leadership skills can achieve sustainable but only moderate success. People with good leadership but poor managerial success can achieve short-term success but long-term failure. Only good managerial skills combined with good leadership skills can lead to sustainable and high success. If you are good at applying the tools and techniques you can achieve moderate success, but to be truly effective as a project manager you need to be a good leader as well.

Table 1.2   Combining management and leadership for success (after Parry 2004)

		Leader	
		Poor	*Good*
Manager	*Poor*	Fail	Dysfunctional: short-term appearance of success; long-term failure
	Good	Sustained but only moderate success	Sustained and high success

This concept is reflected in a model of competence developed by Lynn Crawford (2007), based on the work of Richard Boyatzis (1982). This model will be described fully in the next chapter. She suggests that competence is not just the application of knowledge and skills, the application of the tools and techniques. Competence also encompasses appropriate traits, behaviours and temperament. Yes, a project manager must have what Lynn Crawford calls input competencies, the ability to apply the tools and techniques effectively. But if that is all they can do, it makes them just an adequate manager. To be an inspiring leader (and effective manager) they must also have what Lynn Crawford calls 'core personality characteristics', or 'personal competencies'. In this book we will explain the nature of these personal competencies, and show how they can be developed and improved.

But the nature of these personal competencies is not the same on every project. Somebody who is an effective project leader on one project may not be on another; somebody who is good at bullying subcontractors to deliver on a construction project many not be very good at communicating with and motivating stakeholders on an organizational change project. We aim to describe the nature of different leadership styles appropriate on different types of projects.

There is also the question about whether you are born with these personal competencies or whether they can be learnt. Our view is that you are born with your basic personality profile, but it can be developed, adapted and enhanced. Organizations need to be aware of the types of projects they undertake, and develop project managers with appropriate competency profiles to manage their projects. They should recruit people with a reasonable match, but then through their careers develop those people to become better and better at leading the organization's projects. Further, as we shall see, larger, more complex projects may require different leadership styles than the simpler projects on which those projects managers are likely to start. Thus, organizations must aim to enhance the profiles of their project managers as they develop through their careers. Likewise, project managers must be aware of the types of projects undertaken by the organizations they work for, and look to develop appropriate competencies.

STRUCTURE OF THE BOOK

In the next chapter, we explore the competence model of leadership, and review what has been written over the past eighty years about the traits and behaviours of effective leaders. We compare the general management and project management literature, and show that whereas in the general management arena people have suggested different leadership profiles are appropriate in different circumstances, that is not the case in the project management field, where people have been constrained by the two beliefs introduced at the start of this chapter into thinking that all project managers can manage all projects. In Chapter 3, we focus on the competence school of leadership. In Chapter 4 we then show how this applies to the managers of different types of project and describe a model for profiling the competency of effective leaders. In Chapter 5 we describe different applications of leadership on projects in practice. Chapter 6 integrates the ideas from the earlier chapters and develops a theory of project performance based on the leadership competencies of the project manager.

CHAPTER 2

MODELS OF LEADERSHIP COMPETENCE

Our proposal is that the projects manager's competence, including his or her leadership style, contributes to project success, and that different profiles of competence are appropriate for different types of project. In order to explore this proposal, we need to understand what we mean by competence, and investigate what has been written on leadership competence. In a general management context, it has been shown that the manager's competence, including his or her leadership style, contributes to the success of what they are managing, and different leadership styles are appropriate in different situations, and so we expect that the same would be true for projects. Also, understanding the models used in a general management context provides a perspective through which we can explore the leaders of projects.

In this chapter we begin by introducing a model of competence, and then review how thinkers on leadership over the last 80 years have investigated the different components of the model. We identify several perspectives of leadership, and show what has been written in a general management context, but also how these perspectives have been reflected in writings on project management.

A MODEL OF COMPETENCE

Figure 2.1 shows a model of competence developed by Lynn Crawford (2007), based on a substantial review of the competence literature. There are three components of competence, each consisting of several elements or dimensions of competence.

Input Competence

The first elements are called input competencies, and are the knowledge and skills required to perform the role being undertaken, whether an artisan role, a professional role, a management role, a leadership role, or two or three of those combined. Knowledge will be in the form of explicit knowledge or implicit knowledge, (Nonaka and Takeuchi 1995). Explicit knowledge is reflected in qualifications obtained. Implicit knowledge, which is related to skills, is primarily reflected through experience gained in similar roles.

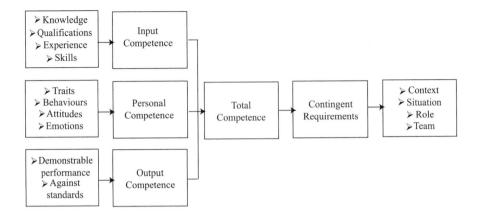

Figure 2.1   Components of competence (Crawford 2007)
Source: Reproduced from *Gower Handbook of Project Management*, Gower Publishing, Aldershot, 2008.

Personal Competence

Personal competence is much more inherent. People bring with them certain traits, behaviours, attitudes and emotional responses to situations which affect their performance. A question that is constantly asked is whether leaders are born or made. You are born with a genetic tendency to adopt certain traits, behaviours, attitudes and emotional responses, and those are then shaped further by your upbringing, and the society and culture within which you are raised. So you are born (and raised) with a certain profile of personal competencies. But then, through further education and training, and through personal development, both conscious and subconscious, you can change your personal profile to better match the society and context within which you are living and working, and thereby improve your performance. So leaders are born with a profile, but they can modify it to improve their leadership ability in different circumstance. But you can only change it so far, and so may be a good leader in some circumstances and not in others.

Output Competence

Output competence is the ability to perform in accordance with the requirements of the role being undertaken, whether an artisan, professional, management or leadership role, or two, three or all four together. The requirements may be defined by standards, which may be:

- *occupational standards* as defined by trade bodies or national vocational qualifications;

- *professional standards* as defined by bodies such as the Association for Project Management, International Project Management Association or Project Management Institute;
- *organizational standards* such as job descriptions.

Total Competence

Total competence is composed of input, personal and output competence.

Contingent Requirements

The performance requirements of the role will be different in different circumstances, that is, they will be contingent on the circumstances. Features of the situation which will change the performance requirements will include the external context, the nature of the situation itself, the nature of the role being undertaken and the nature of other people in that context, including subordinates and other team members.

PERSPECTIVES ON LEADERSHIP

Table 2.1 overleaf, shows how writings on leadership from the past 80 years have reflected this competence model. It shows what has been written in a general management context, and how that has been reflected to date in a project management context. Very little has been written about the input competencies of leadership, which is more than management component of the manager/leader role, but all the other components of the competence model have been covered. We will review each element in turn, and finish by introducing an integrated model which will form the basis of the following chapters. But first we would like to take a small historical aside, reflected in the first line of Table 2.1

Historical Perspectives

Confucius: First we go back to ancient China and Confucius. Confucius identified four virtues (de) leaders should possess, (Collinson et al. 2000):

- relationships (*jen*, love),
- values (*xiao*, piety),
- process (*li*, proper conduct),
- moderation,(*zhang rong*, the doctrine of the mean).

We shall see that in the writings from the last 80 years there has continued to be a focus on people and relationships, values and vision, and following due process. What recent writings have forgotten about is the doctrine of the mean, sometimes called the Goldilocks principle. Confucius thought the leader should take a balanced

Table 2.1   Perspectives on leadership

Perspective	Period	Main idea	Example authors	Project context
Historical perspectives	500 BC	Relationships, values, process, moderation	Confucius	
	300 BC	Relationships, values, process	Aristotle	
Traits	1930s–1940s	Effective leaders show common traits Leaders born not made	Kirkpatrick and Locke (1992)	Turner (2009)
Behaviours	1940s–1950s	Effective leaders adopt certain styles or behaviours Leadership skills can be developed	Blake and Mouton (1978) Tannenbaum and Schmidt (1988)	Turner (2009) Frame (2003)
Emotions and attitudes	1990s–2000s	Emotional intelligence has a greater impact on performance than intellect	Goleman et al. (2002)	Lee Kelly and Leong (2004) Dolfi and Andrews (2007) Clarke and Howell (2009)
Outputs	1930s–1990s	Two styles Transformational: concern for relationships Transactional concern for process	Barnard (1938) Bass (1990)	Keegan and den Hartog (2004)
Contingency	1960s–1970s	What makes an effective leader depends on the situation	Fiedler (1967) House (1971)	Turner (2009) Frame (2003)
Integrated model	2000s	Effective leaders exhibit certain competencies, including traits, behaviours and styles Emotions, intellect, process Certain profiles of competency better in different situations	Dulewicz and Higgs (2005)	Turner & Müller (2006)

approach. But modern managers tend to do everything in extremes. Whatever the flavour of the month is they follow avidly: up-sizing; down-izing, right-sizing; left-sizing. Then when next month a new fad comes along, out it all goes and the new fad is followed avidly. Rather than recognizing that some elements of the old fad were excellent and laying the excellent elements of the new fad over the old, the old is chucked out completely and the new one embraced completely until another fad comes along. Confucius suggests a more balanced approach.

Aristotle: We go forward 200 years to ancient Greece. Aristotle also suggested that the managers should build their relationship with their team in three consecutive steps:

- build relationships (*pathos*);
- sell their values or vision (*ethos*);
- persuade with logic (*logos*).

Unfortunately many managers leap in at the third step, trying to persuade with logic: 'You have to do this, because ... because ... because I am the manager'. Perhaps that is a difference between an adequate manager and an inspirational leader, the manager knows what has to be done and how and why. The leader knows that first they must build relationships with their team, and sell their values and vision to lead the team rather than just push them.

Personal Competencies

Over the years, people have treated the dimensions of personal competence separately, looking at traits, behaviours and, most recently, emotions and attitudes.

Traits: People began exploring the traits of effective leaders in the 1930s. More recently Kirkpatrick and Locke (1991) suggested that effective leaders exhibit the following traits:

- drive and ambition;
- the desire to lead and influence others;
- honesty and integrity;
- self-confidence;
- intelligence;
- technical knowledge.

Through his work at Henley Management College in the UK, Rodney Turner identified seven traits of effective project managers (Turner 2009, first edition 1993).

- *Problem solving:* The purpose of every project is to solve a problem for the parent organization, or to exploit an opportunity (which also requires a problem to be solved). But projects also entail risk, and so during every project you are very likely to encounter problems. Project managers must be able to solve them.
- *Results orientation:* Projects are about delivering beneficial change. But if you plan in terms of the results your plan is much more robust and stable

than if you plan in terms of the work to be done. Thus project managers need to be focused on results.

- *Self-confidence:* This is part of a project manager's emotional intelligence. They must believe in themselves and their ability to deliver. We shall explore this later.
- *Perspective:* Project managers must keep their projects in perspective. A project manager must be like an eagle. They must be able to hover on high and see their project within the context of the parent organization. But they must have eagle-eyed sight to be able to see a small mouse on the ground, and to be able to sweep down and deal with it, but then also be able to rise again to hover above the project.
- *Communication:* And the project manager must be able to talk to everybody from the managing director down to the janitor. Sometimes the janitor knows more about project progress than anybody else, because he or she talks to everybody.
- *Negotiating ability:* Project planning is a constant process of negotiation. As a project manager you ask people to work for you. You must convince them that it is worthwhile and beneficial for them to do that.
- *Energy and initiative:* And when the project gets into trouble, the project manager must be able to lift everybody else onto his back and carry them out of the hole.

Behaviours: Most of the work on behaviours characterizes leaders by how much they exhibit styles based on one or more of the following parameters:

1. concern for people or relationships (*jen, pathos*);
2. concern for production or process (*li. logos*);
3. use of authority;
4. involvement of the team in decision-making (formulating decisions);
5. involvement of the team in decision-taking (choosing options);
6. flexibility versus the application of rules.

Blake and Mouton (1978) developed a two-dimensional grid based on concern for people and production, and identified five types of leader (see Figure 2.2). They suggest that four of the five styles are appropriate in different circumstances; the impoverished style is never appropriate.

Tannenbaum and Schmidt (1958) looked at the use of authority, and suggested a one-dimensional line that snakes its way through the Blake and Mouton grid. There is increasing use of authority from impoverished leaders to country-club and team leaders, with authority-obedience leaders having the greatest use of authority.

Davidson Frame (2003) and Rodney Turner (2009) have suggested four styles of project leaders (see Table 2.2), depending on the extent they involve the team in

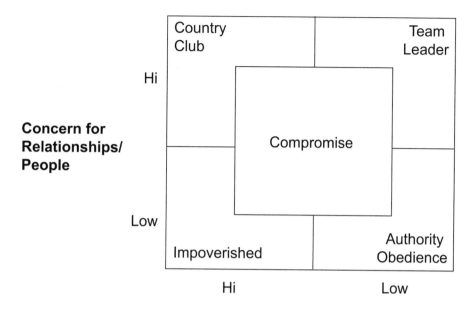

Figure 2.2   The Blake and Mouton Grid (after Blake and Mouton 1962)

Table 2.2   Four styles of project leadership

Parameter	Laissez-faire	Democratic	Autocratic	Bureaucratic
Team decision-making	High	High	Low	Low
Team decision-taking	High	Low	Low	Low
Flexibility	High	High	High	Low

decision-making, in decision-taking, and how flexible they are. They suggest the four styles are each appropriate at different stages of the project life-cycle (see Table 2.3), and with different types of project team.

Laissez-faire style: This style is appropriate at the research or feasibility stage of a project. On a research project the project team members will be leading experts in their field. The project manager can only guide, suggest and lead. He or she cannot instruct. Also when a contracting company is bidding for work, the bid manager will often be junior in strict hierarchical terms to some of the other team members, who may include the contracts manager, engineering manager and potential project manager. Again the bid manager can only guide and not instruct. The other team members respect his or her expertise, and take the guidance, but won't accept

Table 2.3   Project leadership styles, project team types and the project life-cycle

Leadership style	Stage	Team type	Team nature
Laissez-faire	Feasibility	Egoless	Experts with shared responsibility
Democratic	Design	Matrix	Mixed discipline working on several tasks
Autocratic	Execution	Task	Single discipline working on separate tasks
Bureaucratic	Close-out	Surgical	Mixed working on a single task

orders. The team type is called egoless; it is not a forum for the project manager to express his or her ego, nor anybody else, as THE boss.

Democratic: In the design stage of the project, the team includes several professionals, people who are experts in their field, but now junior to the design manager. Several different professionals may each contribute to the design of different parts of the end deliverable (the new asset being delivered by the project). Their relationship with the design of the product is as a matrix, each member of the design team contributing to the design of several parts of the end deliverable. The team members are the experts; they will formulate the decisions. But since several different professionals are contributing to each part of the facility, the manager has to set the overall strategy, and take the final decisions about what will happen. The manager listens to what the team members have to say, but then rules on the final decision.

Autocratic: During the construction phase, the project team members are formed into task forces, each task force building a different part of the plant. The manager needs to be autocratic. Time for discussion is over. The facility is being built and it must be built as designed. Changes cost money, and so the team members must just do as they are told.

Bureaucratic: During the close-out stage of the project, the team forms into a single task force to tidy up all the loose ends. The project manager is like a surgeon in a hospital, leading a team working on a patient. The manager must now be bureaucratic. There are many check lists to be completed, work to be finished off, inspections and tests to be done. The manager must make sure that ticks are put in all the right boxes, and closely follow the procedures to make sure that happens according to the rule book.

Emotions and attitudes: Goleman et al. (2002) suggest all managers have a reasonable level of intellectual intelligence (IQ). They suggest that to do an MBA course requires an IQ of 115. Thus many of the traits and behaviours above are necessary conditions of effective leadership, and will be shared by all inspiring leaders. But they will also be shared by many people who are not good leaders. What differentiates good leaders is not necessarily their intellectual intelligence, but their emotional response to situations. Goleman et al. (2002) identify 19 emotional competencies grouped into four dimensions (see Figure 2.3).

1. personal competencies:
   - self-awareness
   - self management
2. social competencies:
   - social awareness
   - relationship management.

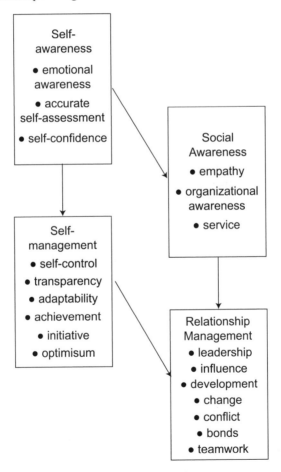

Figure 2.3   Competencies of emotional intelligence

Figure 2.3 shows that we start with self-awareness. Being self-aware we can do two things: self-management and become socially aware. From these two we can progress to relationship management.

Goleman et al. (2002) identify six management styles, exhibiting different profiles of their nineteen competencies. There are four positive styles:

- visionary
- coaching
- affiliative
- democratic.

and two that they describe as toxic styles:

- pace-setting
- commanding.

Through a survey of 2,000 managers, they identified situations in which each style works best. The first four have preferred situations, but all four work in most contexts in the medium to long term. They suggest that the two toxic styles will work in turnaround situations, where rapid recovery is necessary. But if they are applied in a routine environment they will cause adverse reactions in the people being led. The two project managers from the construction company who were transferred to manage an internal change project (Introduction) probably had either a pace-setting or commanding style. Projects are short term, and so you can apply these styles from project to project. But even though an organizational change project is short-term, they don't work for such a project.

To date, very little work has been done setting project leadership within the context of the emotional intelligence school. A research project sponsored by the Project Management Institute (PMI®) was recently completed at Southampton University (Clarke and Howell 2009). However, a contribution was made by Liz Lee-Kelly and Leong (2003) almost by chance. They were researching how the project managers' competence at managing five of the nine PMI PMBoK® knowledge areas contributed to project success. (The five areas they were investigating were scope, organization, quality, cost and time, as defined by Rodney Turner, 2009.) What they found was that there is a significant relationship between the leader's perception of project success and his or her personality and contingent experiences. Thus the inner confidence and self-belief from personal knowledge and experience are likely to play an important role in a manager's ability to deliver a project successfully. The project manager's emotional intelligence, his or her inner self-confidence, has a significant impact on their competence as a project leader, and hence on project success. This is further supported by the work of Dolfi and Andrews (2007) who showed that the project manager's optimism grows with experience.

Output competencies

Work on output competencies has focused on different types of leader, and mainly those who lead by focusing on process and those who focus on relationships. We drew attention to this when discussing Aristotle; there are people who manage through due process, and inspirational leaders who lead by forming relationships and inspire by selling their vision. But we will see later that both are appropriate leadership styles in different circumstances.

Chester Barnard (1938) identified two types of chief executive of companies – those who manage by process and those who focus on relationships and communicate their values – which he called cognitive and cathectic respectively. Bernard Bass (1990) identified two similar styles, which he calls transactional and transformational respectively. Transactional leaders emphasize contingent rewards, reward followers for meeting targets, manage by exception, and take action when tasks are not going to plan. Transformational leaders exhibit charisma, develop vision, engender pride, respect and trust, provide inspiration, motivate by creating high expectations and model appropriate behaviour, give consideration to the individual, pay attention to followers and gives them respect and personality. Furthermore they provide intellectual stimulation and challenge followers with new ideas and approaches.

Bernard Bass (1990) assumes that transformational leaders are always best, but as we shall see this is not the case. Anne Keegan and Deanne den Hartog (2004) assumed that project managers need a transformational leadership style, and set out to show that to be the case. In the event they found a slight preference for transformational leadership, but not a strong preference. We think the reason for this is that complex projects need a transformational style, but less complex projects need a more conscientious, structured style. This has been borne out by the research described in Chapter 4.

Contingency

As we have seen, most of the authors investigating the components of competence assume that different styles are appropriate in different circumstances, but that was formalized by the contingency perspective. Contingency theories tend to follow the same pattern:

- assess the characteristics of the leader;
- evaluate the situation in terms of key contingency variables;
- seek a match between the leader and the situation.

One contingency theory that has proved popular is path-goal theory (House 1971). The idea is the leader must help the team find the path to their goals and help them in that process. Path-goal theory identifies four leadership behaviours:

- supportive leaders
- participative leaders
- achievement-oriented leaders
- directive leaders.

The first three are similar to the positive styles identified by Goleman et al. (2002) and the fourth to their toxic styles. House (1971) suggests that the appropriate style will depend on the nature of the situations and of the subordinates.

AN INTEGRATED MODEL

The integrated model attempts to identify the traits, behaviours and emotional competencies of effective leaders, and then develop profiles for different types of leaders and the way they perform. It then attempts to identify different profiles appropriate in different circumstances. After a review of the literature on leadership competencies, Vic Dulewicz and Malcolm Higgs (2003) identified 15 competencies which influence leadership performance (see Table 2.4). They group the competencies into three types: intellectual (IQ), managerial (MQ) and emotional (EQ).

In Table 2.4, we have shown how the leadership competencies might apply to Confucius's four virtues (*De*). Dulewicz and Higgs also identified three leadership styles for organizational change projects, which they called Goal Oriented, Involving and Engaging (see Table 2.4). The goal-oriented style is similar to the transactional style, and the engaging style similar to the transformational style. Through a study of 400 managers working on organizational change projects they showed *goal oriented leaders* are most effective on low complexity projects, *involving leaders* on medium complexity projects and *engaging leaders* are best on high complexity projects. Thus, Dulewicz and Higgs (2005) showed that on organizational change projects:

- certain leadership styles lead to better results than others;
- different styles are appropriate depending on the complexity of change;
- transactional leaders are appropriate for simple projects and transformational leaders are appropriate for complex projects (with inspirational leaders on medium complexity projects).

We describe the 15 leadership competencies suggested by Dulewicz and Higgs in more detail in Chapter 3, and their model forms the basis for our suggested leadership profiles of project managers in Chapter 4.

Table 2.4   Fifteen leadership competencies (after Dulewicz and Higgs 2003)

Group	Competency	Confucius	Goal	Involving	Engaging
Managerial (MQ)	Managing resources	Process	High	Medium	Low
	Engaging communication	Relationships	Medium	Medium	High
	Empowering	Relationships	Low	Medium	High
	Developing	Relationships	Medium	Medium	High
	Achieving	Values	High	Medium	Medium
Intellectual (IQ)	Critical analysis and judgement	Moderation	High	Medium	Medium
	Vision and imagination	Values	High	High	Medium
	Strategic perspective	Moderation	High	Medium	Medium
Emotional (EQ)	Self-awareness	Moderation	Medium	High	High
	Emotional resilience	Moderation	High	High	High
	Intuitiveness	Moderation	Medium	Medium	High
	Sensitivity	Relationships	Medium	Medium	High
	Influence	Relationships	Medium	High	High
	Motivation	Relationships	High	High	High
	Conscientiousness	Values	High	High	High

PERSONALITY AND TEAM BEHAVIOUR VERSUS LEADERSHIP STYLE

That concludes our explanation of the competence model of leadership. In the next chapter we describe how the integrated perspective applies in a project context. But before we leave this chapter, we would like to differentiate between leadership styles, and personality factors and profiles for team behaviour. Several personality profiles have been developed to explain performance in teams, for instance the Myers-Briggs Type Indicator (Briggs-Myers 1992), the 16PF (personality factor) profile (Cattell et al. 1970), and profiles by Merideth Belbin (1986) and Charles Margerison and Dick McCann (1990). These authors suggest a team leader should aim to balance personality types across a team. Don't have a team made up entirely of Belbin's completer-finishers, because you won't have anything to complete, and don't have a team made up entirely of plants because all you will have is a bunch of bright ideas and you won't be able to begin to sift the wheat from the chaff. You need a balance of Belbin's eight personality types across the team. (Belbin's eight team roles are shown in Table 2.5, together with two more, the specialist and comic, added by Rodney Turner 2009.)

Some people (incorrectly) put the team behaviour profiles forward as leadership styles, indicators of success as a leader. They are not intended for that. Dulewicz and Higgs (2003) have shown there is no correlation between Belbin's personality profile and performance as a leader, and only weak correlation between the 16PF personality factors. Goleman et al. (2002) also address the issue. They say a person's emotional intelligence is a measure of their personality, but their success as a leader is not dependent on their personality but on the leadership style adopted. A person

Table 2.5   Classification of team roles (after Belbin 1986)

Team role	Characteristics	Contribution
Plant	Creative, imaginative, unorthodox	Solves difficult problems
Resource investigator	Extrovert, enthusiastic, communicative	Explores opportunities, develops contacts
Coordinator	Mature, confident, good chairperson	Clarifies goals, promotes decision making, delegates
Shaper	Challenging, dynamic, enjoys pressure	Overcomes obstacles through drive
Monitor-evaluator	Sober, strategic, discerning	Sees all options, judges accurately
Team worker	Cooperative, mild, perceptive, tactful	Listens and builds, reduces conflict
Implementer	Disciplined, reliable, conservative	Turns ideas into practical actions
Completer-finisher	Painstaking, conscientious, anxious	Searches out omissions, delivers on time
Specialist	Single-minded, self-starting, dedicated	Provides scarce knowledge and skills
Comic	Unflappable, robust, resilient	Relives tension

is born with their personality, but they can vary their leadership style by drawing on different emotional competencies depending on the circumstances. They can also learn to develop different leadership styles to suit different circumstances by developing their emotional competencies.

CHAPTER 3

DIMENSIONS OF LEADERSHIP COMPETENCE

In this chapter we present the dimensions of leadership competences associated with the integrated model introduced at the end of Chapter 2. We describe each of the three clusters – managerial, intellectual and emotional leadership competences – and their 15 underlying components. We start with the managerial competences (MQ), which are the bedrock of leadership. Table 1.2 suggested that leadership without management is dysfunctional, and so this competence cluster is an essential foundation of good leadership. We then describe the intellectual (IQ) and emotional (EQ) clusters. The intellectual competences address the cognitive and rational leadership aspects, and the emotional competences the interpersonal and social aspects.

MANAGERIAL LEADERSHIP CLUSTER (MQ)

The managerial leadership dimensions of competence resemble the most traditional understanding of management, which is, guiding and controlling people for the effective achievement of objectives. The historical roots of this cluster go back to the behavioural perspective of leadership, which is concerned with generic leadership styles that lead to superior results. Within the triad of managerial, intellectual and emotional competences the managerial competences address the basic leadership behaviour. The cluster of managerial competences consists of five dimensions: managing resources, engaging communication, empowering, developing, and achieving. We start with the theoretical roots of this cluster.

The Behavioural or Style Perspective and its Relationship with the Managerial Leadership Cluster

The behavioural or style perspective was introduced in Chapter 2. It is concerned with a leader's default orientation and the associated leadership styles. At the most basic level this includes the leader's people versus task orientation.

The importance of that is described by Judge et al. (2004b) who assessed leadership research done in a series of studies at the University of Ohio. It showed that leaders with a people orientation are known for showing *consideration* of the people they lead. These leaders emphasize interpersonal relations, mutual respect and caring for the needs of those being led. Along with that they foster friendship and trust and are more likely to compromise goal accomplishment than relationships with subordinates. Contrarily, leaders with a task orientation are more likely to prioritize task accomplishment over good interpersonal relationships. Their leadership style often emphasizes the *initiation of structures* through processes, policies, reporting channels and others. This research has contributed to the development of a wider number of leadership theories on generally good leadership behaviour, including those by Blake and Mouton (1978), Tannenbaum and Schmidt (1958), and Hersey and Blanchard (1988). (We met Blake and Mouton in Chapter 2.) These theories suggest that there are a few key factors which are generally important for leadership behaviour, including the way leaders:

- plan, organize and control resources, set goals, divide and allocate work and provide feedback;
- are approachable and communicate with their subordinates;
- delegate autonomy to those being led and help them to grow along their individual career aspiration;
- take risks and decisions for the benefit of the project or organization.

These factors are reflected in the five elements in this managerial cluster of competence.

Research by Rodney Turner and Ralf Müller (2006) on the impact of project managers' leadership style on project success showed that these managerial competences are significantly correlated with project success when looking at the sum of all projects, no matter what project type, geography, complexity, performance and so on.

We now discuss these five dimensions of managerial competence and their link to the success of different types of project.

Managing Resources

Managing resources and motivation are the two outstanding leadership characteristics; together they explain about 9 per cent of the success across all projects (Turner and Müller 2006). The developers of the competence model, Vic Dulewicz and Malcolm Higgs (2005, 111) describe this element as:

> *Plans ahead, organizes all resources and coordinates them efficiently and effectively. Establishes clear objectives. Converts long-term goals into action plans. Monitors and evaluates staff's work regularly and effectively, gives sensitive, honest feedback.*

At first glance this reads like a list of traditional management tasks. However, in the sense of a leadership competence, there is no defined level of planning or any other specification about the extent these tasks should be performed. They should be performed to the extent they support efficiency in leadership.

Planning is a typical management task. The extent and contents of planning needed for a leader to be effective vary by leadership style. People-oriented leaders typically plan for environments that allow teams and individuals to make best use of their capabilities and ramp up to highest levels of performance. Examples include research departments, where independence from rigid organizational processes and flexibility in interaction are needed for people to be creative and innovative (Elkins and Keller 2003). In this context, planning emphasizes the end product or service and less of the process of how to get there. This is different for task-oriented leaders. They achieve efficiency through clearly planned processes, policies and other structural support for execution of well-understood tasks. Examples include repetitive maintenance projects, with clearly defined scope and tasks, often executed in competitive markets with low profit margins. However, related examples also include high-risk environments, where failure has to be avoided through strict compliance with defined procedures such as in manned space exploration projects, or the building, upgrade and operations of nuclear power stations. These are just a few, but they are representative for projects requiring high reliability in execution of tasks.

Organizing resources, establishing their goals, developing action plans, as well as performance monitoring, evaluation and feedbacks are also linked with the leader's leadership style. People-oriented leaders will organize the work along the (potential) capabilities of resources and relate performance appraisals to expected outcomes and results, whereas task-oriented leaders will emphasize compliance aspects and organize as well evaluate performance along these regulative aspects of leadership. Both approaches are potentially successful when used in the right circumstances. Effective leaders in projects with well-understood tasks, high risk for mistakes, but small margin for failure, will most likely employ a task orientated leadership style. On the other hand, effective managers in projects with a high level of innovation, unclear project objectives and possibly unknown methods to achieve the goals, will provide freedom for creativity and 'room-for-error' for people to gain experience and learn from their mistakes. The leader's challenge is to assess the situation correctly before deciding for a particular way of managing resources, taking into account the circumstances, tasks, goals, constraints and resources. This decision is crucial for effective leadership and potentially for project success. Neither can creativity be enforced through strict compliance with organizational policies, nor can complex and risky tasks, for which appropriate processes are known, be executed more efficiently by letting people experiment with them. The particularities in managing resources are not a matter of personal choice; they must fit to a project's situation.

Engaging Communication

Our research showed that engaging communication is important in successful projects. By looking at projects of above average performance, we found this dimension to be increasingly important for project success. So in successful projects, where project management appears to be done well, the project managers' communication capabilities are a key factor for project success. Furthermore, engaging communication is of significance in projects of medium complexity, and innovation and maintenance projects, that is, when existing products or services are further developed or even new products for new markets are created (Turner and Müller 2006). Dulewicz and Higgs (2005, 111) describe a leader with this competence as:

> *A lively and enthusiastic communicator, engages others and wins support. Clearly communicates instructions and vision to staff. Communications are tailored to the audience interests and focused. Communication style inspires staff and audiences, conveys approachability and accessibility.*

This definition addresses three different dimensions of communication, namely availability for communication, setting the stage for mutual exchange, and finding the right level of communication detail.

Availability addresses the physical and mental preparedness for communication with others. Effective leaders do this by allowing subordinates to get in contact with them. Once a contact is made they foster a climate for friendly and open communication.

Setting the stage for mutual exchange fosters a stimulating and encouraging exchange by listening, soliciting information, and evaluating information obtained from different perspectives, then combining it with one's own opinions, and discussing these in the light of each person's individual objectives as well as joint objectives. This includes discussing, negotiating and agreeing interesting and challenging goals. The *Theory of Communicative Action* (Habermas 1987) identifies a state of optimal communication, which is reached when there are no mental blockages between communication partners. These blockages are triggered by, for example, differences in authority or reputation of the communication partners, and should be removed through open and empathetic communication.

However, this is not limited to verbal communication. Body language plays a large role in setting the stage for being perceived as an authentic leader of integrity. The unity of words, posture, and actions contribute to the perception of integrity and credibility of a person. Allan and Barbara Pease (Pease and Pease 2005) and Paul Ekman (2004) (www.paulekman.com) are well-known researchers in this area. They did extensive research on a variety of body-language signals which indicate whether a person is talking openly, is trying to hide information, or even telling lies. Among the well-known signals that may convey a negative attitude in a given situation are crossed arms or the hand supporting the head, as well as micro movements in the face of liars. Effective leaders are observant for these signals and use them to adjust their communication style to their audience. These adjustments take into account people's desires by reading their body language in form of, for example, body angles or foot pointing. The former reveals a whole spectrum of interpersonal attitudes, which must be interpreted in a given situation, such as from confrontational attitudes via face-to-face approaches (180-degree angle) to friendly shoulder-to-shoulder (90-degree) angles when standing next to each other. Foot pointing indicates where people want to go (maybe the door) or with whom they are interested to communicate.

The third dimension addressed in this competency is the level of detail in communication. The art of communication lies in finding the right amount and type of information to communicate for a given audience. Research, for example by Tom Burns and G. M. Stalker (1994) has shown the need for speakers to adjust (or aggregate) their information to the level of understanding of the receiver. Where this rule is ignored, for example when technical managers talk jargon to business managers in a project steering-committee meeting, the receiving party (the business managers) will disengage from the communication. They may not be willing to attend similar meetings in the future (Burns and Stalker 1994). The Theory of Communicative Action describes this as *communication breakdown* and identifies it as the most frequent reason for people to stop communicating in business settings. Communication should be phrased in terms of *social correctness*, so that receivers can understand it. Good examples are politicians. The higher they climb in the governmental hierarchy the more slowly and more clearly they speak. This slowdown in the pace of their speaking is not because they age so fast, but because they want to be understood by those they lead.

Empowering

Dulewicz and Higgs (2005, 111) define an empowering leader as someone who:

> *Gives staff autonomy, encourages them to take on personally challenging demanding tasks. Encourages them to solve problems, produce innovative ideas and proposals and develop their vision and a broader vision. Encourages a critical faculty and a broad perspective, and encourages the challenging of existing practices, assumptions and policies.*

Empowerment motivates subordinates. It contributes to perceptions of meaningfulness, autonomy, and perceived impact on results (Kirkman et al. 2004) which are important psychological factors both at the level of teams as well as individuals.

Empowering teams contributes strongly to work-related results, such as customer satisfaction and process improvement (Kirkman et al. 2004). However, implementing empowerment is not done simply by soliciting team-member input and delegating authority. Research has shown that team members are initially sceptical about management's commitment to the new work order. Management's action is seen from the perspective of old work habits and too much similarity between old and new ways of doing work creates scepticism and frustration. Continuing dialogue between management and team members is needed to create plausibility and belief in the new work processes, just as managers need to continually check the fit between team member expectations and their fulfilment. During the implementation of empowerment, team members watch management more closely, because they are sensitive to management's actions (Labianca et al. 2000). Barnard (1999) suggests three aspects that need special attention when implementing empowerment:

- Sharing of information with everyone, but being selective with information in order to avoid information overload. Sharing is needed to build trust and responsibility among team members. However, the shared information needs to be carefully selected for team members to be perceived as useful, and accompanied by useful feedback to the team members about their performance and their overall fit into the team.
- Collaborative development of structures of autonomy. This includes the joint definition of roles and responsibilities, as well as goals and performance measures for each goal, to allow team members to identify where they are in the team. In addition, team members should understand the support, resources and other help that is available for them.
- Replacing hierarchy with empowered teams. This includes continual provision of guidance, training and support, while at the same time, gradually loosening control. This does not imply abandoning control, rather reducing it to the minimum level needed for people to work autonomously.

Especially important in empowerment are virtual teams. Kirkman et al. (2004) showed that the number of face-to-face meetings has a moderating effect on the relationship between empowerment and work results. Fewer face-to-face meetings fosters the strong correlation between empowerment and work results, while more face-to-face meetings decreases the impact of empowerment on work results in virtual teams.

This is supported by our own research, which showed that higher levels of empowerment do not necessarily lead to project success. Worse, they can even be detrimental to success in organizational change projects, or in projects based on time and material contracts or cost reimbursement contracts. Giving too much freedom to team members within projects that involve considerable interactions between people, or where clients pay daily or hourly fees, can easily lead to missing project goals. In these projects careful observation and control of the appropriate level of empowerment is needed (Müller and Turner 2006).

Developing

This competency pervades many different perspectives of leadership. Goleman et al. (2002) refer to this as the bolstering of others' abilities through feedback and guidance, and regard it as one of the sub-dimensions of relationship management in their model for emotional intelligence. Dulewicz and Higgs (2005, 111) define a leader with developing competence as one who:

> *Believes others have potential to take on ever more-demanding tasks and roles, encourages them to do so. Ensures direct reports have adequate support. Developed their competencies, and invests time and effort in coaching them so they contribute effectively and develop themselves. Identifies new tasks and roles to develop others. Believes that critical feedback and challenge are important.*

Project success depends on motivated project team members. One way to achieve motivation is by giving team members the chance to develop themselves, amongst others, by growing their skills, authority, reputation and so on. Research has shown that people perceiving their employers as investing in their development show higher job satisfaction and commitment, and a lower intent to leave the organization (Lee and Bruvold 2003). Developing people within projects is often seen as one of the intrinsic rewards. These rewards exist through the task itself and are not generated externally, via payment or fringe benefits. Intrinsic rewards relate positively to project success in terms of client satisfaction and perceived quality (Mahaney and Lederer 2006).

Research within project management leadership has shown that this competency is especially important for success in IT projects and mandatory projects. Successful leaders apply this competency to let their team members develop in their area of specialization. In mandatory projects, (projects that are required by law and do not necessarily support the company's strategy), the chance for development may be one of the very few options to motivate people to join the project team and engage to the level needed to be successful (Turner and Müller 2006).

The fixed duration of projects and the limited choice of the tasks to be executed severely constrain the breadth of opportunities for development of team members within projects. Companies using project-oriented organization structures often provide little room for employee development within projects. Collaboration between line managers, HR department and project managers is advocated to develop a suitable strategy for the development of employees (Huemann et al. 2007, Bredin and Söderlund 2006).

However, some developments are also possible at the project level. Work done by Anthony Mersino (2007) suggests the following:

- *Acknowledge strengths and contributions of project team members* in order to encourage and motivate them. He suggests finding the particular strengths of each team member and then assigning them tasks that make use of the specific combination of each individual's strengths.
- *Give targeted feedback*, as an investment to team members. While positive feedback is easy to give, care has to be taken when providing feedback on areas for improvement. So he suggests you stick to the facts and be objective, focus on the positive, but also be as clear and accurate as possible, in order to help the person to develop.
- *Provide mentoring, give timely coaching, and offer assignments that challenge and foster a person's skills.* A mentor in this context acts like a trusted friend, counsellor, or more experienced person. A coach teaches and directs via encouragement and advice. Mentoring and coaching can both be done formally and informally. The appropriateness of one over the other depends on the leadership situation and should be carefully evaluated. The assignment of work is a key role of project managers. When assigning work to people, the project manager decides whether to give an individual room to grow or limit the person to his or her existing role. Criteria for this decision should include the short- and long-term needs of the project and the individual, as well as the possible need for cross-training to reduce risks in resource bottlenecks or potential savings stemming from the flexibility of individuals in the team.

Developing others requires a balance between the needs of the project, the individual and the wider organization. As a leadership dimension it draws on the interpersonal and inter-organizational capabilities of the leader and his or her understanding of the wider organizational issues.

Achieving

Dulewicz and Higgs (2005, 111) defines a leader with achieving competence as one who is:

> *Willing to make decisions involving significant risk to gain an advantage. Decisions are based on core business issues and their likely impact on success. Selects and exploits activities that results in the greatest benefits to the organisation and its performance. Unwavering determination to achieve objectives and implement decisions.*

Achieving is about striving optimistically for continuous improvement of performance. It is one of the main factors distinguishing average from superior performers. The latter take on more calculated risks, are open and supportive for innovations, set challenging goals for their team members. A key factor for achievement is optimism, because it influences preparatory actions and reactions to unfavourable events. Leaders with high achievement competencies are more proactive and persistent; they have an optimistic attitude towards setbacks and act from the perspective of success (Goleman 2001).

Complementary to these attitudes are activities. These start with the identification of the key issues to be addressed and their associated critical success factors. Actions following these identifications integrate circumstances, issues and critical success factors for the benefit of the outcome. Risks are calculated carefully, but are taken if the circumstances allow for success. Thinking and action are results-driven.

Research by Dulewicz and Higgs (2005) showed that high achievement leaders are best suited for delivering results in relatively stable contexts. Their style is leader-led and appropriate for stable organizations in circumstances where deliverables are well understood. In these situations, little disturbance and distraction from the environment can be expected. This allows the project manager to centralize the leadership role within themselves and to focus the efforts on project outcomes and results.

INTELLECTUAL LEADERSHIP CLUSTER (IQ)

The intellectual competence cluster addresses the cognitive and rational side of leadership. Intelligence has always been perceived as a trait of successful leaders. The historical roots of this assumption go back to early leadership theories, such as the trait perspective.

The Trait Perspective and its Relationship with Intellectual Leadership Competencies

This perspective looks for traits – the distinguishing features or characteristics – of a leader. Numerous studies have supported the perception that intelligence, typically in form of cognitive and rational capabilities, is indeed a trait of successful leaders. Along this line of thinking, measurements of intelligence have long been used as a predictor for people's success in business. These tests were originally developed to measure school children's cognitive capabilities to predict success in school. Later they were adapted to for adults and used in a wide variety of settings, including the selection of people for jobs, as well as for predicting managerial success in organizations. These tests were based on the assumption of a linear relationship between cognitive capabilities and success.

As early as 1973 McClelland questioned the validity of intelligence measures alone for predicting people success, and suggested measuring competences instead of cognitive capabilities only. He suggested the inclusion of personality characteristics like communication skills, patience, moderateness in goal setting, and the ego of an individual in addition to his or her cognitive capabilities (McClelland 1973). In continuation of these developments Goleman (1995) refined this thinking into his formula EQ + IQ = success. Shortly afterwards Dulewicz and Higgs (2000) started to develop the integrated competence model, which includes not only the intellectual, emotional and managerial capabilities, but also the related skills for executing these capabilities, thus competences.

During that time the development of the trait perspective did not stop. Later research in this perspective indicated that cognitive capabilities of successful leaders are typically above average, but not brilliant. Despite these findings, intelligence remains as one of the main traits followers look for in their leaders. Consequently it becomes a source of authority for the leaders (Kirkpatrick and Locke 1991).

A meta-study by Judge et al. (2004a) on the relationship between cognitive capabilities and leadership showed that people perceive the link between cognitive capabilities and leadership to be stronger than quantitative evidence suggests. Subjective opinions on the importance of high IQ for leadership success seem to be overestimated. Quantitative evidence showed only a moderate strength of the relationship. So the link is neither strong nor trivial. The intelligence–leadership relation is also not static in its nature. Along with cognitive resource theory (Fiedler and Garcia 1987, cited in Judge et al. 2004a) the meta-analysis showed that cognitive capabilities and leadership performance are more strongly related when leaders are:

- Exposed to lower levels of stress. This happens because stress diverts leaders' attention away from the task at hand, because they start to worry about possible failures and question their self-efficacy, instead of staying focused on planning and decision making;
- When leaders exhibit directive behaviour. This communication style allows for communicating plans and associated tasks unequivocally. If intelligent leaders make better decisions, then this communication style enables those being led to receive the benefits of these decisions.

So it is more important to put intelligent individuals in management positions when stress levels are low and the leader has a chance to be directive (Judge et al. 2004a).

But why is intelligence important for managers? The need for cognitive capabilities arises from the need of leaders to acquire, process and analyze a large amount of information, then judge upon the results of the analyses and develop a creative vision, and a strategy to implement this vision.

Those who score high on Vision, Strategic Perspective and Critical Analysis have the intellectual ability to perceive the context and the degree of change in organizations more widely and accurately (Dulewicz and Higgs 2003). We now describe these three dimensions.

Critical Analysis and Judgement

This competency lies at the heart of managerial activities. It supports the manager in the day-to-day assessment, evaluation and judgement on the variety of different types of information that are needed in fulfilling the project manager role. Dulewicz and Higgs (2005, 111) define a leader with this competency as one who:

> *Has a critical faculty that probes the facts, identifies advantages and disadvantages and discerns the shortcomings of ideas and proposals. Makes sound judgment and decisions based on reasonable assumptions and factual information, aware of the impact of any assumption made*

This definition describes critical analysis and judgement as comprising analytical skills which are needed for assessment and evaluation of various types of information. At the same time it requires the ability to identify realistic criteria for analysis and to relate these to different context parameters. This includes, for example, the judgement on a possible project delay, given the different information from team members and suppliers, and the judgment on the impact of such a delay. This provides the basis for a subsequent analysis of various scenarios, which take into account factors internal and external to the project in order to come up with best possible solution in the given circumstances.

A review of the research literature on the leadership – intelligence relationship showed that this intelligence is perceived as the most common factor among leaders. While certainly important for every management role, our own research shows that this particular competency does not appear to be especially important for success in most project types (Turner and Müller 2006).

Vision and Imagination

This competency relates to one of the oldest principles of leadership, which is, being creative and setting a vision for others to follow. Dulewicz and Higgs (2005, 111) define leaders strong in this competency as:

> *Imaginative and innovative in all aspects of one's work. Establishes sound priorities for future work. Clear vision of the future direction of the organization*

to meet business imperatives. Foresees the impact of changes on one's vision that reflect implementation issues and business realities.

Creativity is required to develop or anticipate the organization's role and outcomes in the market. In terms of projects this translates into being creative in how to achieve the project objectives, the products or services to be created through the project and the related priorities.

Vision consists of three elements, which build on a solid set of core values and beliefs of an organization. These are (Collins and Porras 1991):

- A purpose, which states the type of business the organization is in and the reason for its existence. In projects this is the 'raison d'etre' of the project and its business case.
- A tangible image of the product or service to be created, often in form of a compelling mission statement, written in a way people can mentally adapt to it.
- A vivid description of the desired end-state, such as an accomplishment or the benefits of using a new product. In project contexts the description and the image define the scope and outcome of the project.

Finally, this competency includes the ability to anticipate changes and the impact of changes on the project and its vision.

Vision and imagination are important for the organization and possibly also for project results. However, research has shown this dimension relates negatively to project success when used by the project manager. One explanation for that phenomenon might be that the vision for the project should be articulated by the project sponsor, not by the project manager. The sponsor sets the objectives and should therefore also define the vision for the project outcome. A further explanation is that an overly imaginative project manager may be tempted to introduce frequent changes to the plans and scope of a project, which would be detrimental to project success. This is in line with research findings on conscientiousness – an emotional intelligence competency – which is described later in this chapter. These findings indicate that successful project managers are very conscientious about their work and keep a low profile on their creative and visionary capabilities (Turner and Müller 2006).

Strategic Perspective

The strategic perspective addresses the manager's ability to see the big picture and evaluate the impact of changes, risks and stakeholders on decisions and tasks in projects. A leader strong in strategic perspective is defined by Dulewicz and Higgs (2005, 111) as one who:

Sees the wider issues and broader implications. Explores a wide range of relationships, balances short- and long-term considerations. Sensitive to the impact of one's actions and decisions across the organization. Identifies opportunities and threats. Sensitive to stakeholders' needs and the implications of external factors on decision and actions.

This competence should not be confused with the recent attempts to shift project work from the operational into the strategic domain of an organization (Thomas et al. 2002, Jugdev et al. 2009). These approaches take an organization-wide perspective and suggest planning projects and project management as a strategic capability of the firm.

As a leadership competency strategic perspective relates to project success in different ways across different types of projects. One constant in *general* projects is that this dimension tends to constrain project success. Too broad a picture and an overly strategic perspective on the part of the project manager hinders the project. As in the case of vision and imagination, it seems that the wider perspective is better adopted by the sponsor rather than the project manager; over-sensitivity towards stakeholders and the likely impact of change may encourage scope creep and the risk of missing of project objectives.

However, in *IT projects* the project manager's capabilities for strategic perspectives relate positively to project success. In the context of these projects, the project manager should take on a wider perspective, be more sensitive to stakeholder needs and the likely impact of project changes than they should in the case of other projects (Turner and Müller 2006). This dimension is more sensitive to project type than any other.

The three competencies from the Intellectual Intelligence cluster described above represent the competences for the rational and cognitive dimensions of leadership in the competence perspective.

EMOTIONAL LEADERSHIP CLUSTER (EQ)

The cluster of emotional competences addresses the interpersonal and social dimensions of leadership. Our research identified this set of competences to be highly correlated with project success across all types of projects. Within high-performing projects, the correlations increased with the extent to which the project delivered physical products. Purely product related projects, such as engineering and construction projects showed the highest correlation between emotional competences of the project manager and project success. Projects made up of both products and new processes, such as IT projects showed a less strong correlation; and projects involving mainly process and people related contents, such as organizational change projects, showed the least correlation between emotional competences of the project manager and project success (Turner and Müller 2006)

Early works on emotional intelligences and competences date back to the1950s, but the subject had its breakthrough in 1995 with Daniel Goleman's book *Emotional Intelligence*. Since then the topic has experienced a strong growth in interest amongst both academics and practitioners. The word *emotion* is of Latin origin and means *move away*. It refers to individuals' immediate and non-cognitive reaction to events, such as a threatening situation. Psychologists define eight basic emotions. These are anger, sadness, fear, enjoyment, love, surprise, disgust and shame. Emotions are mainly steered by the amygdala, a nut-size circuitry located in the middle of either side of the brain, whereas the more rational tasks are regulated in the prefrontal area of the brain. The emotional part works faster than the rational part of the brain. Immediate reactions are therefore mostly driven by the amygdala, which 'thinks' holistically, in pictures and feelings, while the rational part works much slower and 'thinks' analytically, logically, in abstract and cause-effect relations (Goleman 1995).

A number of different theories on emotional intelligence have been developed over the years. We describe the most influential ones.

The Emotional Intelligence Perspective and its Relationship with Emotional Leadership Competencies

Intelligence generally refers to the mental abilities for handling of and reasoning about information. The emotional intelligence perspective in particular refers to a person's ability for accurate reasoning about his or her emotions and the use of emotions and emotional knowledge to enhance thought. Three streams of research developed in recent years (Mayer, et al. 2008):

- *Specific ability approaches* include research for better understanding of specific skills fundamental to emotional intelligence, such as accurate interpretation of facial expressions, gestures and body language. Furthermore it includes research on how emotions facilitate thinking or behaviour of people, how emotions are accurately labelled and classified, and how they are managed.
- *Integrative model* approaches link several dimensions of emotional intelligence into an overall model. This includes the four-branch model of Mayer and Salovey (1997), which links abilities from four areas: a) accurately perceiving emotions, b) using emotions as a facilitator of thought, c) understanding emotions, and d) managing emotions.
- *Mixed-Model* approaches include research on emotional intelligence in a broader sense, often in relation to other personality traits, such as those from the traits perspective.

The most popular model was developed by Daniel Goleman, Richard Boyatzis and Annie McKee (2002) and comprises the management of oneself and ones relationship with others. Emotional intelligence is thus assessed along the four dimensions of self-awareness, self-management, social awareness and relationship management (Figure 3.3). In their definition emotional intelligence refers to how leaders handle themselves and their relationships. Emotionally intelligent leaders drive the emotions of those they led by creating resonance between the leader and those being led. That creates emotional 'buy-in' to the subject, and eases acceptance of interactions at the rational level.

Building on his prior work and a number of business cases that support his model, Daniel Goleman (2001) developed an EI–Based Theory of Performance. The theory is grounded in the four dimensions listed above plus their sub-dimensions, Table 3.1. The balance of recognition and regulation for both the individual and others creates synergies and allows the different dimensions of competence to support each other. Star performers demonstrate strengths in at least six of these sub-dimensions and in at least one of each of the four clusters.

Table 3.1   Framework of emotional competencies (after Goleman 2001)

	Self **(Personal Competence)**	**Other** **(Social Competence)**
Recognition	Self-awareness • Emotional self-awareness • Accurate self-assessment • Self-confidence	Social awareness • Empathy • Service orientation • Organizational awareness
Regulation	Self-management • Self-control • Trustworthiness • Conscientiousness • Adaptability • Achievement drive • Initiative	Relationship management • Developing others • Influence • Communication • Conflict management • Leadership • Change catalyst • Building bonds • Teamwork and collaboration

The emotional intelligence perspective with its focus on the ability to read, understand and manage oneself and ones relationships with others reflects the thinking underlying the emotional competencies cluster. Due to its focus on competences and not only intelligences, the distribution of the different sub-dimensions varies from the emotional intelligence model of Goleman. Most of the emotional competences overlap. However, some sub-dimensions from the Goleman model are found in the intellectual and managerial competencies clusters of the competency perspective. The emotional competencies of the competency perspective are discussed next.

Self-Awareness

Dulewicz and Higgs (2005, 112) define this competence as:

> *Awareness of one's own feelings and the capability to recognize and manage these in a way that one feels that one can control. A degree of self-belief in one's capability to manage one's emotions and to control their impact in a work environment.*

Self-awareness is about recognizing a feeling as it happens. Daniel Goleman (1995) refers to it as the keystone of emotional intelligence – the ability to monitor feelings at any moment, crucial for psychological insight and self-understanding. It includes the awareness of one's moods and the related thoughts about the moods. Mayer and Stevens (1994) showed that clarity about one's emotions, and the associated better knowledge about the own boundaries, leads to being more autonomous, having a positive outlook, and good psychological health.

Self-aware leaders monitor their inner signals. They are conscious about the impact their feelings have on their performance at work. They recognize anger early, before it has built-up and is close to an outburst. Furthermore, they analyze potential causes for anger and develop a constructive reaction to it. By being aware of one's own feelings, the leader is easily tuned into how others feel and can act empathetically, which is the basis for building resonance among people. Leaders lacking emotional self-awareness often loose their temper without knowing why their emotions push them around (Goleman et al. 2002).

Project managers' self-awareness is especially important in maintenance projects, when existing products or services are to be improved, as well as in projects with fixed price contracts. In these circumstances we saw a strong positive correlation between project managers' self awareness and project success (Turner and Müller 2006).

Emotional Resilience

Emotional resilience is required for dealing with pressures, conflicts and time demands that often accompany changes (Mordaunt and Cornforth 2004). It allows controlling emotions while under pressure, and thereby facilitates or enables high performance (Dulewicz and Higgs 2004). A person with emotional resilience is defined by Dulewicz and Higgs (2005, 112) as one who:

Performs consistently in a range of situations under pressure and adapts behaviour appropriately. Balances the needs of the situation and task with the needs and concerns of the individuals involved.

Resilience refers to a person's ability to recover rapidly after experiencing some adverse experience. A person strong in this competency behaves emotionally competently across many stressful experiences. Emotional resilience emerges from the emotional competence of a person, but is also influenced by his or her relationships with others. A person high on emotional resilience can cope with stressful situations within his or her capacity to cope with stress. Challenging tasks may even extend this capacity, but should be consistently supported by the resources the person draws from in their social relationships (Saarni 2000).

Daniel Goleman (2001) argues that emotional resilience allows a person to remain comfortable with the level of anxiety that often accompanies uncertainty. Such a person shows ongoing creativity to achieve desired results. A person lacking this ability may be resistant to change, slow to respond to market changes, and hinder new and innovative ideas.

The importance of the link between resilience and social competences was also identified by other researchers. They argue that higher levels of both emotional resilience and social competences increase the ability to better withstand the stresses of life and the temptations to become involved in self-damaging behaviour, such as taking drugs (Topping et al. 2000).

In a project context emotional resilience is needed for coping with the unexpected shortcomings and drawbacks that accompany unique endeavours. Emotionally resilient project managers recover from these events quickly enough to stay 'on top' of the situation, with sufficient overview to push forward to developing new and innovative solutions to the problems at hand. At the same time they are flexible enough to adapt to changing situations and constructively change the project to the new, often unexpected, circumstances.

Emotional resilience appears to be especially important in IT projects. A study by Williamson et al. 2005) showed that this competency accounts for almost 20 per cent of job satisfaction and career satisfaction of IT professionals. Our own studies supported the importance of this competency for IT projects, but also for organizational change projects. Medium complex IT and organizational change projects showed a strong correlation between emotional resilience and project success (Turner and Müller 2006).

Intuitiveness

A person with intuitive abilities is defined by Dulewicz and Higgs (2005, 112) as one who:

> *Arrives at clear decisions and drives their implementation when presented with incomplete or ambiguous information using both rational and 'emotional' or intuitive perceptions of key issues and implications.*

Intuitiveness links rational thinking with gut feeling. One supports the other. Business-related data and information, often collected in data warehouses, knowledge databases or other decision support systems, provide the general alley for a decision. However, our gut feelings, whether we feel good or bad about a possible decision, often influence the final decision made. Goleman et al. (2002) refer to these feelings as the accumulation of life-long experiences. The brain accumulates learning from all decisions taken during one's life and associates them with feelings. Decisions that were successful in the past are associated with good feelings and unsuccessful decisions with bad feelings. In a decision making situation the brain searches for and brings back the feelings associated with similar decisions in similar circumstances. These feelings are used as a set of data, in addition to rational data available for decision making. Especially important is intuition in decisions with little reliable information, such as decisions about future products and services in dynamic markets.

Intuition is therefore increasingly important for higher levels of management, where decisions about the future must be made on the basis of little or no reliable information. (Dulewicz and Higgs 2003). That explains why results from research on the importance of intuitiveness at lower levels of the organizational hierarchy are inconsistent. While many studies support the importance of intuitiveness for success in business, a study by Higgs (2004) showed that intuitiveness correlates negatively with performance in UK call centres. So intuitiveness can even be detrimental to performance in some roles. So the project manager needs to try to be aware when it is appropriate in himself or herself, and in the project team, and when a more structured, conscientious approach may be required.

That is in line with our own research, which identified intuition as the only competency that was not significantly higher in managers of high performing projects when compared with managers of low performing projects. With the exception of intuitiveness, all competencies were expressed significantly higher in those managers managing projects at or above the average performance level of all projects, when compared with managers of projects below the average performance level. Accordingly, intuitiveness did not surface in our analysis of competencies as being needed for project success. The only exception was during the early phases, the feasibility stage of projects. Here intuitiveness appears to correlate with project success due to ambiguity of the situation and the lack of reliable information for the new and unique endeavour called project. (Turner and Müller 2006).

Interpersonal Sensitivity

Interpersonal sensitivity is closely linked with empathy, shown when interacting with others. Dulewicz and Higgs (2005, 112) define a sensitive person as one who:

> *Is aware of, and takes into account, the needs and perceptions of others in arriving at decisions and proposing solutions to problems and challenges. Builds from this awareness and achieves the commitment of others to decisions and action. A willingness to keep open one's thought on possible solutions to problems and to actively listen to, and reflect on, the reactions and inputs from others.*

Interpersonal sensitivity comprises the ability of being attuned to the impact one's own words have on the person receiving them (Goleman1995). A person's ability in empathy, which goes along with sensitivity, provides for the awareness of others' emotions, concerns and needs. He or she reads from verbal and non-verbal cues, such as tone of voice or facial expressions. It is a critical factor for performance in professions that require a high level of interaction between people, such as physicians, R&D managers, or retailers. Moreover, interpersonal sensitivity allows for accurate interaction and avoidance of stereotyping when dealing with people (Goleman 2001). Research by Dreyfus (2008) showed that sensitivity distinguishes highly effective from typical managers. Their capability develops early on in their life. Many of the sensitive leaders are aware of their abilities by the time they complete college. They develop these capabilities through positive and negative experiences in interactions. Related behaviour includes:

- listening and taking into account others' point of view by acknowledging, but not necessarily agreeing to what they say;
- recognizing the needs of others;
- appreciating effective relationships with others;
- stimulating a spirit of co-operation.

A lack of interpersonal sensitivity often leads to hurtful interactions, which can cause bitterness, defensiveness and distance (Goleman 1995). Research by Witt et al. (2002) showed that lack of interpersonal sensitivity, even within highly conscientious workers, may lead to ineffectiveness, particularly in roles that require interaction with others. Our own research indicates a strong positive correlation between interpersonal sensitivity and project results in:

- all high-performing projects;

- engineering and construction projects for repositioning;
- IT projects for renewal of existing products or services;
- all projects based on fixed-price contracts;
- all highly complex projects.

Thus it confirms the importance of interpersonal sensitivity for projects with intensive interaction among people.

Influence

Influence is about shaping the outcomes of interactions (Goleman 2006). As a competence, influence makes use of a synergetic effect between self-awareness, which helps to read and control one's own emotions, interpersonal sensitivity, which allows reading other people's emotions, and knowledge about the legitimacy of different actions in the given situation. When exercising influence, leaders impact situations in several ways. Their formal position as a leader makes followers listen to their words and opinion about a subject. Their ability to control emotions by displaying self-control in confrontational situations enhances trust and respect among the followers. Interpersonal sensitivity and empathy, as the ability to understand other people's emotions, allows the leader to adjust to the feelings of followers and find 'the right tone'. This combination allows a leader to effectively influence the feelings of others, and thereby their reaction (Gardner and Stough 2002).

Dulewicz and Higgs (2005, 112) define an influential leader as one who:

> *Persuades others to change views based on an understanding of their position and a recognition of the need to listen to this perspective and provide a rationale for change*

Goleman et al. (2002, 265) say that:

> *Indicators of a leader's powers of influence range from finding just the right appeal for a given listener to knowing how to build buy-in from key people and a network of support for an initiative. Leaders adept in influence are persuasive and engaging when they address a group.*

Influence is practised by being persuasive and managing the emotions of others. This is done by sensing the emotions of others and responding carefully to move an interaction towards a desired outcome. Leaders strong in this competence have the ability to impress others, often through dramatic effects, but without strong force, and appeal to reason and rational decisions (Goleman 2001). In his book on social intelligence, Daniel Goleman (2006) describes the example of a police officer who is just writing a ticket for double-parking when the car owner comes up loaded with emotions. By calmly giving the advice that it would be better to get into the car and drive away than to continue to discuss the issue until the police officer calls the tow-away service, an appeal to reason is made and the car owner follows the advice.

Influence is exercised in project management when the project manager uses the formal power of their role to make team members or other stakeholders listen, then tune into their emotions and convey his or her own position on an issue, and finally appeal to the rationality of a given solution. To that end it mirrors Aristotle's process of pathos, ethos, and logos from 300 BC.

Project managers' influence competence relates positively with project success in organizational change projects which are either highly complex or executed solely within the home culture of the project manager, on remeasurement contracts, and in the feasibility and commissioning stages of the project life-cycle (Turner and Müller 2006).

Motivation

Motivation is one of the classic themes in management. Examples include Abraham Maslow's (1943) hierarchy of needs, and Frederick Herzberg's (1987) theories on motivational and hygiene factors, or Paul Hersey and Kenneth Blanchard's (1988) situational leadership theories. The theory of transformational leadership builds on motivational factors to increase commitment and productivity of followers. Dulewicz and Higgs (2005, 112) define a motivational leader as someone with:

> *Drive and energy to achieve clear results and impact. Balances short- and long-term goals with a capability to pursue demanding goals in the face of rejection or questioning.*

The importance of motivation derives from both the impact of motivation on a person's own performance as well as the effect on other people's motivation and their performance. People lacking motivation may not only perform below their own capabilities, but also influence others negatively, and with that the team's overall performance. Motivation is therefore seen as a critical factor for leadership (Ghosh and Chakraborty 2007).

Motivation as a concept is measured and defined in different ways. For example, some researchers refer to *what* motivates people, others to the general *mood* and its impact on self-motivations, whereas a third group refers to the *outcome* of the former two. An example for the first group includes Kirkman et al. (2004), who distinguish between intrinsic and extrinsic motivators. Intrinsic motivators consist of a variety of factors embedded in the task itself and rooted in the set of tasks, responsibilities and capabilities. Team motivation is hereby achieved when team members hold high perceptions about the team's *potency* to master the tasks, the *meaningfulness* of work, the required *autonomy* to carry out the work, and the significance of the *impact* of the results. Extrinsic factors, on the contrary, originate from outside the team. These include rewards, evaluations, recognition from externals, feedback from stakeholders, customers, peers, as well as peer pressure and team norms. Examples for the second and third group of motivation researchers include those looking for:

- *self-motivation*, as measured by the Bar-on (2006) emotional intelligence test. Here motivation is linked to optimism, that is, the extent people are positive and look at the bright side of life, and happiness, which refers to people feeling content with oneself, others and life in general.
- *drive* and *energy* to attain challenging long-term goals or targets (Dulewicz and Higgs 2004).

Goleman (1995, 89) states that 'positive motivation – the marshalling of feelings of enthusiasm, zeal, and confidence – in achievement', is a unifying trait of world-class musicians, athletes and chess grand masters. It derives from coupling ones dreams about life with a task at hand, which provides for continuous energy and commitment (Goleman et al. 2002). From a brain scientist perspective Goleman (2001) concludes that motivation is steered by the brain through holding in mind or reminding positive feelings associated with attaining personal goals and at the same time allowing inhibiting the negative feelings which discourage from continuing to strive toward those goals.

All these different perspectives towards motivation come together in project management. From providing the project team with meaningful work, autonomy, potential for success, and significant impact on the outcome, as described by Kirkman et al. (2004), via recognizing the mood and self-motivation of individuals within the project as described by Bar-on (2006), towards the development of drive and energy as measured by Dulewicz and Higgs (2004). To achieve that the project manager should link the dreams, ambitions and values of the team members with the project at hand, as described by Goleman et al. (2002).

Our own research showed that motivational capabilities of the project manager correlate positively with project success across all types of projects. The impact increases with the level of people interaction needed. It is lowest in engineering and construction projects, increases in IT projects and peaks at organizational change projects. Furthermore, it is especially important for success in projects of medium complexity, repositioning projects, and engineering and construction projects based on remeasurement contracts.

Conscientiousness

The conscientiousness dimension pervades the majority of theories and measurement models in leadership. As a concept it is found in many of the well-established theories either directly or in combination with other traits. It correlates with personality factors, such as those of the Five Factor Model for Personality (McCrae and John 1995), and is sometimes referred to as 'Attention to detail', such as in Boyatzis et al. (2000). Dulewicz and Higgs (2005, 112) define a conscientious leader as someone who:

> *Displays clear commitment to a course of action in the face of challenges and to match 'words and deeds' in encouraging others so support the chosen direction. Shows personal commitment to pursuing an ethical solution to a difficult business issue or problem.*

Conscientious team members are typically reliable, trustworthy and internalize company norms and values (Williamson et al. 2005). They are consistent in their words and actions and behave in accordance with ethical standards (Dulewicz and Higgs 2004). They are careful, self-disciplined, and take their responsibilities seriously. These are the people who keep things running, often perceived as organizational role models. Outstanding performance in almost all roles can be traced back to conscientiousness (Goleman et al. 2002).

In project management this competence is needed for a variety of tasks, such as paying sufficient attention to the details of planning and execution of projects, establishing team morale and showing ethical behaviour, and last, but not least being committed to deliver the project outcome, even when facing difficulties.

Conscientiousness is a key competence for project management. Our studies showed consistently that project managers of high performing projects had highest levels of conscientiousness. Project managers' conscientiousness and project performance correlated strongly across all high performing projects, all project phases, from design to commissioning and especially strong in highly complex or fixed price engineering and construction projects.

SUMMARY

This chapter reviewed the 15 dimensions of competence associated with the integrated competence model of leadership and associated theories, and related them to a project management context. We outlined contents and importance of each of these competencies and their cumulative and mutual supportive effect at the aggregate level of EQ, MQ, and IQ. The next chapter looks at the personalities of leaders.

CHAPTER 4

PERSONALITIES OF LEADERS

In this chapter we look at the personalities of project managers, the particular personality characteristics of successful project managers in different types of projects, as well as personality differences by roles, such as the line manager role and the project manager role. We briefly address differences by national cultures. The chapter finishes with suggestions on how to develop competent leaders for different project types.

COMPETENCES FOR PROJECT SUCCESS

Our research (Turner and Müller 2006, Müller and Turner 2007a) on the relationship between project managers' leadership styles and project success showed that across all projects, no matter what project type or project performance, the EQ competency of *motivation* and the MQ competency of *managing resources* are significantly related with project success and explain about 9 per cent of a project's success. However, projects are unique undertakings and must therefore be understood at a more detailed level. As a first distinction we chose the difference between high- and low-performing projects, the reason being that projects can fail for many reasons, some of them beyond the control of the project manager. Moreover, if we assume The Standish Group (1998), KPMG (2005) and others are right in their findings that only a fraction of all projects perform as planned, then the majority of the projects we have in our research sample are low-performing. So we need to filter out those projects which we can learn from and understand how projects should be managed in order to be successful and performing. These are the high performing projects. Therefore we looked at those projects whose success measure was at or higher than the average of all projects. Success was measured as the average of success measures listed in Table 4.1.

All but one of the 15 leadership competencies (intuitiveness) are significantly stronger in the managers of successful projects than in the managers of less successful projects. Across *all* high-performing projects the EQ leadership dimensions of conscientiousness and sensitivity, and the MQ dimension of engaging communication, correlate positively with project success. The better the project manager is in these elements of leadership the higher the level of project success.

Table 4.1   Project success criteria and measurement

Project success criteria
End-user satisfaction
Supplier satisfaction
Team satisfaction
Other stakeholders' satisfaction
Performance in terms of time, cost, quality
Meeting user requirements
Project achieves its purpose
Customer satisfaction
Reoccurring business
Self-defined criteria

However, the IQ dimension of strategic perspective is negatively related to success. Possible reasons for that are discussed in Chapter 3. These four competencies explain about 14 per cent of project success in high performing projects.

In high-performing *engineering and construction* projects, two of the 15 leadership dimensions shown in Table 2.4, namely conscientiousness and interpersonal sensitivity, correlate positively, and vision correlates negatively with project success. This combination explains about 43 per cent of the success measures for these projects. So a sense of duty, and awareness of others' needs and perceptions in order to gain commitment, are the project managers' leadership attributes contributing to project success in engineering and construction projects.

In high-performing *IT and Telecommunication* projects it is engaging communication, self-awareness, and developing resources that correlate positively and vision negatively with project success. That explains about 21 per cent of the success measures. We see that the 'soft' factors make IT projects successful. Project managers using the right 'tone' with others, and helping others taking on challenging tasks, together with good control over their own feelings, are the attributes of successful leadership in these projects.

In high-performing *organizational change* projects it is engaging communication and motivation which are positively, and vision which is negatively, related to projects' success. These leadership competencies explain about 17 per cent of the success in these types of projects. Actively creating the required dynamics for change by motivation, and then accommodating the changes through engaging communication, helps organizational change projects to be successful.

Other contexts that foster the importance of specific leadership competencies are listed in Tables 4.2 to 4.4. They show the specific context within which a leadership competency becomes significantly correlated with project success. How to use these tables for training and selecting project managers for specific project types is described in the section on *Developing Competent Leaders* further on this chapter.

Table 4.2   Contexts fostering the importance of MQ leadership competencies

Managerial Competencies

Engaging communication
- IT and organizational change projects
- Medium complexity IT and organizational change projects
- Highly complexity IT projects
- Renewal and repositioning organizational change projects
- Fixed price contracts – especially in organizational change projects
- Feasibility, design, execution and close-out phase of IT and organizational change projects
- IT and organizational change projects in the project manager's home culture

Managing resources
- All project types

Empowering
- (highly complex organizational change projects)
- (Engineering and construction projects under remeasurement contracts)

- Developing
- IT projects
- Mandatory IT and organizational change projects

Achieving

( ) = negative correlation with project success.

Table 4.3   Contexts fostering the importance of IQ leadership competencies

Intellectual Competencies

Vision and imagination
- (Engineering and construction, IT and organizational change projects)
- (Medium complex IT and organizational change projects)
- (Repositioning engineering and construction and organizational change projects)
- (Engineering and construction, and organizational change projects under remeasurement contracts)
- (Feasibility, design and execution phase of IT projects)
- (Feasibility, design and close-out phase of organizational change projects)
- (Organizational change projects in the project manager's home culture)

Critical analysis and judgment
- Renewal engineering and construction projects

Strategic perspective
- IT projects
- (Commissioning phase of IT projects)

( ) = negative correlation with project success.

Table 4.4   Contexts fostering the importance of EQ leadership competencies

Emotional Competencies

Self-awareness
- IT projects
- Renewal projects
- Projects under fixed price contracts
- Design, execution, close-out phases of IT projects
- IT project manager works in his/her home country

Emotional resilience
- Medium complex project

Motivation
- IT and organizational change projects
- Medium complex IT projects
- Repositioning projects
- Engineering and construction projects under remeasurement contracts
- Commissioning phase of projects
- Design phase of IT and organizational change projects

Interpersonal sensitivity
- Engineering and construction projects
- Highly complex projects
- Repositioning engineering and construction projects
- Renewal IT projects
- Fixed-price projects
- Commissioning phase of projects
- Projects in the project manager's home culture

Influence
- Engineering and construction projects
- Highly complex organizational change projects
- Repositioning engineering and construction projects
- Renewal IT projects
- Projects under remeasurement contracts
- Feasibility and commissioning phases of IT projects
- Commissioning phase of organizational change projects
- Organizational change projects in the project manager's home culture

Intuitiveness
- Feasibility phase of IT projects

Conscientiousness
- Engineering and construction projects, especially when highly complex, or under fixed price contract, or in design, execution, close-out, and commissioning phase
- Organizational change projects and engineering and construction projects in the project manager's home culture

Further details about the research results on significant competencies for different levels of complexity, contract types, project importance, project phase and project manager's culture can be found as a larger report (Turner and Müller 2006), or a shorter research paper (Müller and Turner 2007a). Next we look into the different personality types of successful project managers in different types of projects. Before we can do that we need to define personality.

WHAT IS PERSONALITY?

Personality is:

> *the sum of all the attributes – behavioural, temperamental, emotional and mental – that characterize a unique individual (Wordnet 2009).*

These attributes are observable as relatively stable behaviour patterns known as traits. The relative variation in these traits makes people distinct from each other and thereby individual. But where do these traits come from? Building on the work of John Mayer (1995), John Mayer, Peter Salovey and David Caruso (2000) developed a three-level model which explains the emergence of personality traits. The three psychologists define the parts of a person's mind, the interconnections of these parts and the outcomes in terms of personality traits. At the lowest level (Level 1) Mayer et al. (2000) define the four mental processes for motivation, emotion, cognition and consciousness. These are:

- *Basic Motivations*: the inward looking and biological needs of a person, such as those for food, water, safety and so on, which are translated into the related behaviour such as eating, drinking and so on.
- *Basic Emotions*: these are more outward looking processes and include the eight basic emotions listed in Chapter 3 such as joy, sadness, anger and so on.
- *Basic Cognitive Operations*: these most outward looking processes include learning, remembering, judging, comparing and related activities.
- *Basic Consciousness*: this is the person's awareness of the rest of the mind, sometimes defined as creatively changing, interrupting and redirecting mental work in case it is deemed inadequate – for example, a speaker changing his style of talking when he becomes aware of the bored expressions of the listeners.

The same four concepts are frequently used in the emotional intelligence and competence perspectives. The second level of this model shows the mental maps a person develops from the processes at Level 1. The development from Level 1 to Level 2 occurs through learning. By learning from the inward and outward oriented processes of Level 1, the models of Level 2 are developed. Here:

- Basic Motivation and Basic Emotions from Level 1 combine into the *Model of the Self.* This includes a person's understanding of his or her identity, the ideal self, the self-concept and so on.
- Basic Emotions and Basic Cognitive Operations from Level 1combine into the *Model of the Self-in-World.* This includes a person's roles, attachments, identifications, and rules of conduct.
- Basic Cognitive Operations and Basic Consciousness from Level 1 combine into the *Model of the World.* This includes general knowledge how the world functions, such as knowing how to spell, or how to obtain expert knowledge in a particularly area of interest.

It is important to note that the three mental maps at Level 2 don't necessarily reflect reality. The view a person has about himself or herself may be very different from other people's perceptions of that person. The third and highest level of the personality model comprises the mental traits, which are combinations of the models from Level 2. They surface through interaction of a person with others:

- the Model of the Self and the Model of the Self-in-World combine into *Self Relevant Traits,* such as self-esteem, self-consciousness, ego strength and so on.
- the Model of the Self-in-World and the Model of the World combine into a person's *General Traits*, such as extroversion, verbal intelligence, conscientiousness, dogmatism, friendliness and so on.

The model explains personality as stemming from a person's motivation, emotion, cognition and consciousness. These are combined into three pictures of a person and the world. These pictures then shape the nature of the interaction a person has with other people, thus a person's individual personality traits, which are among others expressed in the person's leadership style. Similarities with the emotional intelligence and competence perspectives of leadership are obvious; similar concepts are used and related to a person's behaviour, including the leadership style. Next we expand into the competence school and look at the personalities of successful project managers.

LEADERSHIP COMPETENCY PROFILES OF SUCCESSFUL PROJECT MANAGERS

In our research (Turner and Müller, 2006), we identified the personality and competency profiles of successful project managers of engineering and construction, IT and organizational change projects (see Figure 4.1). At the top and to the right are the IQ competencies, below them on the right the MQ competencies and on the left side of the diagram the EQ competencies.

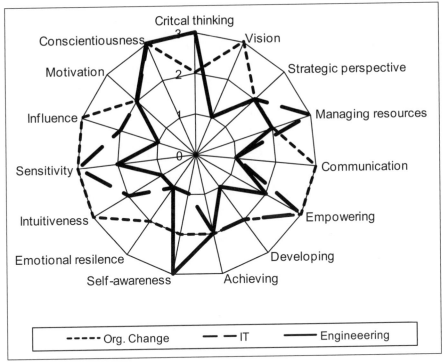

Figure 4.1   Personality profile of successful project managers in different types of projects

The managers of successful engineering and construction projects show strong IQ competencies in critical thinking, and EQ competencies of self-awareness and conscientiousness. The strength of their human-resource-management related dimensions rank medium, and strategic competencies rank lowest. The nature of their projects requires the ability for rational and critical assessment, attention to detail, but also good self-control for proper conduct.

The managers of successful IT projects are strong in the IQ competence for critical thinking, the MQ competencies for empowering and managing resources, as well as the EQ competencies for sensitivity and conscientiousness. Similarities with engineering-project managers are in low levels of vision, communication and emotional resilience. Their low level of self-awareness is in contrast to engineering-project managers. Medium to strong are their strategic and human resource-management-related abilities. The profile lies somewhere between engineering and construction and organizational change project managers, most likely because of IT projects having both a technical as well as an organizational component.

The managers of successful organizational change projects are medium to strong in all competencies. Outstanding is their high level of EQ related competencies.

The intangible nature of their projects' outcome requires strong IQ competencies in vision, MQ competencies in communication, and empowering, as well as EQ competencies for intuitiveness, sensitivity, influence and conscientiousness. Due to the nature of their projects they build vision and objectives, and then influence their environment and their team to change towards these objectives.

So the personalities of successful project managers differ by project type. But how do the personalities differ by role, such a line manager role versus project manager role? In other words, do good project managers fit into line-manager roles and vice versa?

Differences between Line Managers and Project Managers

The first difference is a logical one: we cannot relate line managers' leadership competencies to project results, because they do not manage projects. They manage their resources on a continuing basis. Project managers manage resources in temporary organizations, that is, until the project is finished. So to compare them we need to have a common measurement of performance. Dulewicz and Higgs (2005) have developed a measure for leadership performance which is equally applicable for line managers as for project managers. It measures leadership performance in terms of team members' individual contributions and team output. The questions underlying these measures cover team members' efforts, capabilities, flexibility, team performance and impact.

Profiles for Leadership Performance

Dulewicz and Higgs (2003) maintain a database with the profiles of the 15 leadership dimensions of more than 1,000 line managers. A comparison of the averages of these line managers and the averages of project managers showed that project managers score on average significantly higher than line managers on:

- Critical analysis and judgment (an IQ competency);
- Conscientiousness (EQ);
- Interpersonal sensitivity (EQ).

However, project managers scored significantly lower than line managers in the competencies of:

- Engaging communication (MQ);
- Developing others (MQ).

It shows that the different roles of line and project manager require different personality profiles. Line mangers who transfer in a project manager role must improve their IQ and EQ competencies of critical analysis and judgment, conscientiousness and interpersonal sensitivity, whereas project managers who transfer into line manager roles should improve their MQ competencies for communication and developing others.

The contributions of EQ, MQ and IQ to leadership performance vary also by role. As shown in Table 3.5, leadership performance can be predicted to 71 per cent for line managers by using the EQ, IQ, MQ scales, but only to 31 per cent for project managers. Perhaps this is because projects, as temporary organizations, are impacted much more by external factors beyond the project manager's control.

Recent years have brought a few new project management methodologies, such as SCRUM, XP and others, which are grouped under the name of Agile Methods. These methods change the traditional understanding of the role of project manager from a manager to a facilitator. Research on the leadership competencies of these managers (also known as SCRUM Masters) showed significant differences in the leadership profiles of traditional project managers and agile project managers. According to Porthouse and Dulewicz (2007) agile project managers score significantly:

- higher in intuitiveness, communication, and developing others;
- lower in motivation and conscientiousness.

When comparing agile project managers with line managers, the agile project managers score significantly:

- higher in intuitiveness and interpersonal sensitivity;
- lower in motivation and emotional resilience;

Table 4.5 shows the contribution of EQ, MQ, and IQ to agile project managers' leadership performance, and compares it with traditional project managers and line managers. It shows that leadership performance of line managers can be best predicted (71 per cent) by their leadership competence profile, followed by agile project managers' leadership performance, which can be predicted up to 61 per cent, and traditional project managers' leadership performance, which can only be predicted to about 31 per cent through their EQ, MQ and IQ profile.

This summary of recent research showed the need for different leadership styles in different roles and project types. But how can we find or develop a suitable manager for a given role or project?

Table 4.5   **Predicting leadership performance**

	Line/functional managers (Dulewicz and Higgs, 2000)	Agile/SCRUM project managers (Porthouse and Dulewicz, 2007)	All project managers (Turner, Müller and Dulewicz, 2009)
Individual correlations			
EQ	36%	40%	21%
IQ	27%	4%*	22%
MQ	16%	19%	30%
Aggregate correlations			
EQ	30%	40%	21%
EQ + MQ		58%	
EQ + IQ	52%		26%
EQ + IQ + MQ	71%	62%	31%

* = not significant.

DEVELOPING COMPETENT LEADERS

Line or Project Manager Personality?

People should be carefully chosen for different roles. A first decision should be whether a person is more suitable for a line manger or a project manager role. The measures on leadership performance from Table 4.5 help here. It shows that to achieve leadership performance a certain level of EQ is needed in all managerial roles; however, more so in line manager roles and less in project manager roles. This is consistent with what Daniel Goleman (1995) said, that increasingly higher levels of EQ are needed when moving up the corporate hierarchy. Candidates with high EQ and IQ may be better suited for line manager roles, whereas candidates with strong MQ plus a balance of EQ and IQ may be better suitable for achieving leadership performance in a project manager role. At the more detailed level should the competencies in engaging communication and developing others be assessed and candidates high on these competencies made possible line manager candidates. Similarly those strong in conscientiousness, sensitivity and critical thinking may be better considered for a project management role.

This is in contrast to many organizations' practice of using projects and project management as a training ground for the development of their general managers.

Different leadership competencies are required in different management roles. Accordingly, training programmes for managers should prepare candidates for the particularities of their role. Those pursuing a line management career should be trained to a lesser extent in MQ and IQ dimensions than those pursuing a project management career. Jumping back and forth between project management and line management roles should be done carefully and infrequently. A short-term switch into 'the other role' could be beneficial for broadening the horizon, for example through gaining insight in different organizational processes, or to satisfy a person's job-enrichment desires. However, it should not become a long-term strategy. The personality structures required in different roles vary too much.

Choosing the Right Project Manager for a Project

In fact the decision about whether a person is suitable for the project they are about to be assigned to is not best made when they are about to be appointed to the project. It is best made as they are about to be appointed to the pool of potential project managers the firm should maintain. We would recommend that an organization should maintain a pool of potential project managers, and a career structure for project managers with defined competences to manage the type of projects the organization does at different levels (Turner et al. 2008). The organization will then develop the project managers in the pool through the career structure to manage its projects. To achieve this, we suggest a five-step process:

Step 1: Recognize your types of projects. Awareness is growing that projects need to be categorized for better management. This is evident in organizational developments such as project portfolio management, or industry-specific project management methods such as the Construction Extension of PMIs PMBoK Guide (Project Management Institute, 2007). A state-of-the-art categorization system was developed by Lynn Crawford, Brian Hobbs and Rodney Turner (2005). They distinguish between project attributes, such as application area or complexity, and project types within each category of attributes, such as engineering, IT and organizational change within the attribute category of Application Area. For the research described above we used a subset of these categories, which allowed for 19 different categories of projects (see Table 4.6). The model is applied by choosing one of the project types in the right-hand column for each attribute type. Together this defines the project type.

Having categorized the projects in your organization lays the foundation for the following steps:

Step 2: Assess the leadership styles of your project managers. This step develops an inventory of the leadership styles within the pool of project managers. Many assessment tools are available on the web. We used the Leadership Dimensions

Table 4.6   Simplified project categorization model

Project attributes	Project types
Application area	Engineering and construction, ICT, or organizational change
Complexity	High, medium, or low
Strategic importance	Mandatory, repositioning, or renewal
Contract type	Fixed price, remeasurement, or alliance
Life-cycle stage	Feasibility, Design, Execution, Close-out, Commissioning
Culture	Project manager in single culture, host culture, or expatriate

Questionnaire (LDQ), developed and administered by Dulewicz and Higgs (2005). For contact information send an email to: ralf.mueller@pm-concepts.com. This assessment will provide a profile of each project manager along the 15 leadership dimensions, such as those in Figure 4.1.

Step 3: Develop competence profiles in accordance with project needs. The first criterion for selecting project managers is the project type in terms of application area. Intuitively this makes sense and our empirical research showed that no other categorization had a better explanatory power of the leadership impact on project success. Generally speaking we can say that project managers who are conscientious and encouraging should be selected to lead engineering or construction projects. Their competences are best suited for managing these types of projects because of the need for discipline and due diligence in managing projects through their life-cycles, but also because of the need to integrate various opinions and possible solutions to problems into a realistic project approach. Project managers who are communicative and self-aware, and enjoy leading people, should be considered for IT projects. Their competence profile helps addressing the typical IT project problems of unclear goals and low budgets and excessive expectations from the later users of the system. Energetic and people-oriented managers with strong motivational skills should be considered for organizational change projects. Their drive and interpersonal competencies make them best suitable for a leadership position in these projects.

With the competence profiles of the project managers and the information about project types the 'ideal' competency profiles can now be developed. This is done by identifying whether a project is for engineering and construction, IT, or organizational change. Figure 4.1 shows the targeted profile for project managers managing these projects. Then emphasis is put on having the right competence level in each of the competencies related with project success.

Let's work through an example of a project of the following profile: engineering project, medium complexity, design stage, for renewal of existing products, executed in the project manager's home culture under a fixed-price contract. We apply the following sequence:

From the text above under the title Competences for Project Success we read 'conscientiousness and interpersonal sensitivity correlate positively, and vision correlates negatively with project success'. Accordingly the candidate project manager should have at least the same strengths in conscientiousness and sensitivity as the target profile in Figure 4.1 (that is high and medium respectively). This is the default profile we are aiming for in his project. With the project profile in mind we screen Tables 4.2 to 4.4 for the occurrence of parts of the project profile. Marking these in Tables 4.2 to 4.4 provides us with further leadership competencies for project success, which may be of importance due to the specific leadership context. In the given example, this would be managing resources, vision and imagination, critical analysis and judgement, plus all emotional competencies except intuitiveness. We then screen the competency profiles of our project managers and make sure that the assigned project manager is at least at the same level as the targeted profile in each of the identified competencies. Better even stronger than in the default profile, except vision and imagination, which should preferably be lower than the target profile. Through this process we have identified the best-fit between project type and project manager leadership competence.

It is possible that the existing project managers do not fit with the targeted profile for a project type. Then the required competences (especially those which correlate with project success) need to be developed through training or experience. It is said that IQ is somewhat fixed after the age of 12. EQ and MQ, however, can be developed throughout the entire life of an individual (Goleman 1995). A project manager's leadership style can so be tailored to suit the needs of a particular project type. It increases the likelihood for both project and project manager to be more successful. These developments are of a longer term and require the project manager to define and take deliberate efforts to improve particular competencies. Reading a book on communication does not make a person an 'engaging communicator'. It requires open feedback from co-workers or mentors over an extended period of time, backed-up with training and extensive practice to improve in the desired area. However, the results pay off. Becoming a conscientious, sensitive communicator pays off in engineering projects; being self-aware, coaching and developing others improves IT projects; and having drive and motivational capabilities increases chances for success in organizational change projects.

Step 4: Differentiate different types of projects in the organization. In this step we allow project managers working on the same types of projects (and potentially with a similar leadership profile) to gain from their experiences, or even leverage them. This is done by specific knowledge-sharing events for particular project types, or specific training programs for these types of projects. The introduction of project portfolio-management marks such awareness. Project portfolios are groups of projects in need of the same type of skills. Structuring the organization along portfolios, with the associated targeted training and community of interest events for the resources in a portfolio increases the adaptation of leadership competence needs and developments.

Step 5: Value your project managers. Many organizations complain about their inability to hire good project managers from the market, or the difficulty in keeping those already employed. No wonder! Good leaders are in demand and they have the freedom to choose between organizations. And they choose organizations that value them as leaders and managers of their business and their most valuable assets (their employees), not as someone who only knows how to move a mouse and thinks this is project management (Introduction).

LEADERSHIP IN DIFFERENT CULTURES

So far we have not included national differences in the discussion on leadership. This subject is very broad and goes beyond the boundaries of this book. However, there are a few cultural aspects that should be considered. More details can be found in (Müller and Turner 2007b).

Differences in Importance of Success Criteria

Different cultures assign different weight to the importance of success criteria. Project managers working in their home country are on average more successful with their projects than those working abroad or as expatriate. The rating of success, however, is influenced by culture, because the decision on project success is influenced by the importance assigned to the different project success criteria (see Table 4.1 for the success criteria).

Culture influences the perceived importance of team satisfaction, end-user satisfaction, stakeholder and supplier satisfaction in a project. That explains why project managers working in their home country are often perceived as more successful than those working abroad or as expatriate.

The North American culture emphasizes customer satisfaction over all other criteria, while the European cultures downplay the importance of this criterion. On the contrary the North American culture downplays the importance of supplier satisfaction, when compared with other cultures in the world. When compared with other cultures, the European cultures put lower importance on the satisfaction of end-users, teams and other stakeholders. This is unfortunate, because research has shown that an increase in the importance of team satisfaction, end-user satisfaction and customer satisfaction have a positive effect in reaching all of the success criteria shown in Table 4.1. The importance assigned to team satisfaction is almost universally impacting all success criteria. Through that the team's satisfaction advances to the most important of the success criteria. How is team satisfaction achieved? Through proper leadership; this is the subject of this book.

SUMMARY

In this chapter we addressed the personality of the project manager, identified those leadership dimensions that are important in different roles and different projects, developed a process to choose and develop appropriate project managers for an organization's project types, and finally looked into cultural differences in the perception of project success criteria. The next chapter addresses the practical application of those leadership competencies deemed important.

CHAPTER 5

THE REALITY OF PROJECT LEADERSHIP

A common theme in Chapters 2, 3 and 4 was building relationships with the wider project team, including the team itself, the project sponsor and other stakeholders. In Chapter 4, we saw that managers will try to persuade the stakeholders with logic, whereas leaders will first build relationships with them, then sell their vision, and having gained their commitment, work with the stakeholders to find the best process to achieve the desired objectives. Figure 2.3 shows that building relationships with the project stakeholders is the ultimate aim of the emotionally competent leader, but suggests that first he or she must understand how they are going to react emotionally to situations, and in particular, how they are going to respond to the project. In order to be able to do that the project leader must be able to predict and manage his or her own emotional responses to situations.

In Chapter 3 we saw that there are several dimensions of competence which are important for project leadership. These include conscientiousness, motivation, sensitivity, self-awareness and communication. These competencies are particularly significant for building and maintaining relationships with the stakeholders and project sponsor, winning and maintaining their trusts and avoiding and resolving conflict between them. In this chapter we explore the project managers' leadership role in these areas. But we recall that in the Introduction we said that leadership without management is dysfunctional. The project leader must also be a good project manager. In Chapter 4 we showed that the five managerial dimensions of competence are as significant as the seven emotional dimensions. Thus as we look at the reality of project leadership we find the project leader having to balance both the managerial and leadership elements of their role.

BUILDING RELATIONSHIPS WITH STAKEHOLDERS

Rodney Turner (2009) has suggested that a necessary condition for project success is to agree the success criteria with all the stakeholders before you start. If you can win their support before you start you are far more likely to succeed than if you wait until the end of the project and then begin to think about how to win their support. You are unlikely to win full support of every stakeholder, but if you can make a good stab and by identifying the key stakeholders and earning their respect you are well on the way to project success. To build relationships with stakeholders you need to identify who they are, predict their response to the project and develop a communication plan to interact with them (see Figure 5.1).

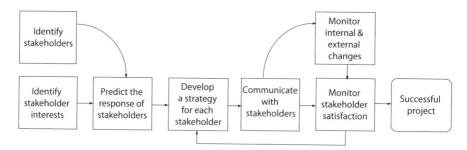

Figure 5.1   Stakeholder management process

Identifying Potential Stakeholders

Identifying potential stakeholders is primarily a managerial dimension. The left-hand column of Table 5.1 suggests potential stakeholders of a project. To illustrate who these might be, consider a project to build a new production plant for a manufacturing company.

The owner or investor is the person or group who are going to pay for the project and receive the benefit from its operation. In our example this is the board of directors of the company and ultimately the shareholders.

The consumers are the people who are going to buy the outputs from the new asset and so provide the revenue that will generate profit and ultimately pay for the new asset the project produces. In our example they are the people who buy the new product.

The operators or users are the people who are going to operate the new asset on behalf of the owner. In our example the production department, represented by the production director.

The sponsor is the person or group who identify the need for the new asset and its potential benefit to the organization, argue for its construction, win resources including funding, and support the project through its delivery. In our example, this is the marketing department, represented by the marketing director.

The project team are the people who will do the work of the project, including the project manager. In our example they may come from the company's engineering department.

Table 5.1   Project stakeholders and their assessment of success against three levels of project results

Results	Project output	Project outcome	Impact
Timescale	**End of project**	**plus months**	**plus years**
Stakeholder			
Owner/investor	Time Cost Features Performance	Performance Reputation Profit Consumer loyalty	Whole life value New technology New capability New competence New class
Consumer	Time Price of product Features	Benefit Price of product Features Developments	Benefit Price of product Features Developments
Operators/users	Features Performance Documentation Training	Usability Convenience Availability Reliability Maintainability	Competitive advantage New technology New capability New competence New class
Sponsor	Completed work Time Cost Performance Safety record Risk record	Reputation Relationships Investor loyalty	Future projects New technology New competence New class
Project team	Time Cost Performance Learning Camaraderie Retention Well being	Reputation Relationships Repeat business	Job security Future projects New technology New competence
Suppliers	Completed work Time and cost Performance Profit from work Safety record Risk record Client appreciation	Performance Reputation Relationships Repeat business	Future business New technology New competence
Public	Environmental impact	Environmental impact Social costs Social benefits	Whole life social cost-benefit ratio

Suppliers are people from outside the company who will provide work, goods and services.

The public is an almost limitless stakeholder, making it almost impossible to identify 'all' the stakeholders. The public may include:

- other people in the company not directly involved on the project;
- people living close to the site of the proposed new factory;
- local, regional, national and continental government;
- pressure groups;
- the media.

You need to be particularly concerned about the media. They are not in business to tell the truth; they are in business to sell newspapers.

Identifying the Interests of Stakeholders

The stakeholders all have different success criteria for the project. Identifying those requires sensitivity to anticipate the stakeholders' use of the project outcome, and empathy to identify their success criteria. Figure 5.2 illustrates a model for different levels of project results, and success of the project is judged against the project results over different timescales.

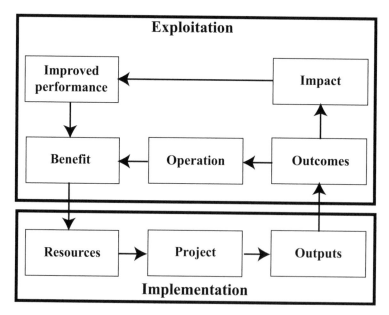

Figure 5.2   Three levels of project results

The project output is the new asset delivered by the project. In our example this is the new production plant. Success against this is judged as the work of the project finishes.

The project outcome is the new capability that operation of the asset gives the organization. In our example this is the ability to make and sell the new product. Success against this is judged in the months following the project.

The impact is the long-term improvement that we will deliver to the organization. In our example this is ultimately increasing profits and shareholder value, but may include the ability to exploit new markets. Success against this is judged in the years following the project.

Table 5.1 shows how different stakeholders assess success against the three levels of project results. There is a vast range of different understanding of what is meant by success, and it can mean that one stakeholder views the project as a success and another as a failure, and people can think the project a success as the work of the project finishes, but think it a failure months or years later, or vice versa. However, if you start in the feasibility stage to identify possible stakeholders, and work to align their perceptions of success, you are more likely to achieve a successful outcome. If you wait until you are about to commission the asset, it is an impossible task. So you must build relationships and sell your vision before you start.

From Table 5.1 we can match different stakeholders to their potential interests. But, 'There is nowt so queer as folk', so don't assume people are necessarily going to behave as you expect. Having identified the stakeholders and formed relationships with them, you need to work with them to try to find out what truly motivates them.

Predicting the Response of Stakeholders

We can now try to predict the response of stakeholders, which is about trying to judge their emotional responses to the project, and so requires the project leader to be empathetic and sensitive. In order to do this, we suggest you ask three questions about each stakeholder:

1. Do they support the project?
2. Can they influence the outcome?
3. Are they knowledgeable about the project?

Table 5.2 will help you answer the first question. But as we said, don't assume people will behave always as expected. A SWOT analysis of each stakeholder

Table 5.2   Stakeholder register

Stakeholder	Objective	For/ Against	Influence level	Knowledge	Influence strategy
Board	Profits	F	Med	Yes	Keep informed
Marketing	New product range	F	Hi	Yes	Maintain sponsorship
Operations	New production facilities	F	Hi	No	Brief, consult to identify needs
Local residents	No pollution or traffic	A	Lo	No	Conduct environmental assessment Inform through local media
Local politicians	Employment in low employment area	F	Lo	No	Brief, win support
Local media	Make a story	?	Hi	No	Inform of benefits to local region and environmental assessment
Environmental activists	Make trouble for chemical industry	A	Med	No	Inform of environmental assessment and jobs benefits Ask politicians to brief
etc					

will help answer the first two questions, (except it is a OTSW analysis). You ask yourself:

- Does this stakeholder view the project as an opportunity? If so, then presumably they support it.
- Does this stakeholder view the project as a threat? If so, then presumably they oppose it.
- What strengths does this stakeholder have to influence the outcome?
- What weaknesses does this stakeholder have that I can use to reduce their threat to the project if they are an opponent, or opponents can use to reduce their influence if they are supporters?

Obviously the people who support the project and can influence the outcome are the ones you are trying to encourage through open and engaging communication, and the ones who oppose the project and can influence the outcome are the ones who put your social skills to test. Remember Aristotle's three step process of pathos, ethos, and logos when approaching them. When emotions are already high also take into account what we said in Chapter 3 about the police officer. Influence is practised by being persuasive and managing the emotions of others. Impress them by describing effects, but without strong force, and appeal to reason and rational decisions.

The answer to the third question determines your communication plan. People who don't yet know about the project should hear about it from you first. We believe that if someone hears about the project as a rumour, on the grape vine, they are likely to be against it. Their reasoning will go something like: I heard about this as a rumour, therefore management must be trying to keep it secret, therefore it must be bad, so I am against it. It is also well known that once people have come to a wrong conclusion based on faulty information, they find it difficult to change their minds once they get correct information. So you don't want people to hear about a good project as a rumour and decide they are against it. You want to be the first to tell them, and give them positive information about the project. And the communication style should, of course be *engaging* to allow the stakeholder to exchange and clarify information.

From a managerial perspective you can record your answers to your stakeholder analysis in a stakeholder register. Table 5.2 is an example for our new production plant above, which is now assumed to be a chemical plant on the edge of a residential area. The last column shows the planned influence strategy, which we will discuss next. The stakeholder register is one of the tools of project management where half the benefit comes from just filling it, helping you think through who the stakeholders are, what their individual concerns are, how well informed they are, and how you will communicate with them.

Influencing the Stakeholders

Influencing is an EQ competency of leaders, described in Chapter 4. There are three management models for planning and preparing our leadership in influencing stakeholders.

Knowledge-attitude influence strategy: The first model is based on whether the stakeholders are aware or ignorant of the project, and whether they support or are against it, Figure 5.3:

- *Aware–support.* These people are your friends. But they must not be taken for granted. Continue to work with them and keep them informed through empathy and engaging communication.
- *Ignorant–support.* These people are expected to support the project when they know what it is about. Be the first to tell them so they gain positive messages about the project and to avoid them slipping into the bottom right box. This again requires the project leader to adopt engaging communication.

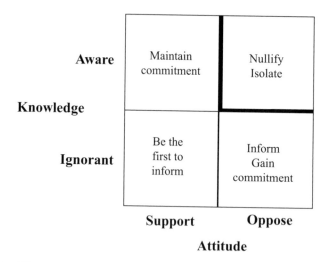

Figure 5.3   The knowledge–attitude influence strategy

- *Ignorant–oppose.* It is very difficult to move these people out of this box. It is a quirk of human nature that if people form an incorrect opinion based on incorrect or incomplete information, they find it very hard to change their mind even when they get correct, complete information. So if somebody starts in the bottom left box, be the first to tell them about the project to move them to the top left. Don't let them move to bottom right based on a rumour, because they may remain against the project for the wrong reasons. It is also important to talk to people in terms they can understand, in layman's language. This requires the project leader to adopt empathy, sensitivity, engaging communications and, probably most important, influence.
- *Aware–oppose.* These people are almost easier to deal with, they are against the project for good reason, and so you can have a rational discussion with them. You either need to find ways of changing the project to win their support, or make sure they can't influence the outcome. This requires sensitivity and engaging communication.

Power–influence matrix. The second model is the power influence matrix, depending on the power of the stakeholder within the organization, and their ability to influence the project. It leads to four strategies (Figure 5.4), but four bands rather than the beloved four quadrants.

Socio-dynamics. The third model is socio-dynamics due to D'Herbemont et al. (1998), and shown in Figure 5.5. It is based on how much the stakeholders are committed to the goals of the project, and how much they accept the method of delivery. They identify many different types of stakeholders.

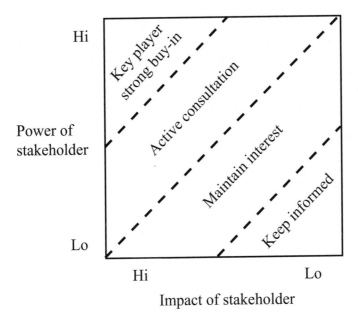

Figure 5.4   Power influence strategy

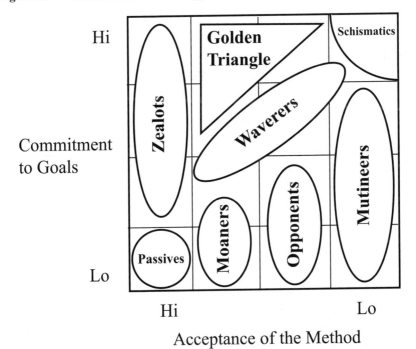

Figure 5.5   Socio-dynamics

The passives represent about 40 per cent to 60 per cent of the stakeholders. The way they flip will depend on which way the waverers flip, and which way they flip will depend in turn on the influence of the golden triangle, so you need to work at strengthening the influence of the golden triangle. You might think that the zealots are your best supporters, but they are just giving blind support. The golden triangle consists of thoughtful supporters and so will have greater influence on others. They are very useful people who basically support the project, and help you to improve it. Over 30 years ago the then member of parliament for the Henley-on-Thames constituency, Michael Heseltine, gave an evening lecture at Henley Management College. He was a Conservative MP, the party then in opposition. At the time the Labour government were putting a bill through parliament that almost everybody supported, but the Conservatives were opposing it in parliament. So during the questions following the lecture somebody asked Michael Heseltine why the Conservatives were opposing this legislation. He said it was because that was their job; they were Her Majesty's official opposition, so it was their job to oppose. Yes, it was good legislation, but there were flaws in the bill as drafted and so by opposing it they made it even better. That is the role of the golden triangle, making the project better by questioning what is being done. It shows the need for empathy and sensitivity. Understanding the role and perspective of the other parties helps to anticipate their behaviour and craft one's own plans accordingly. Being weak in this can have severe consequences, as shown in the next example.

The schismatics are often the previous CEOs who think the new CEO is doing everything wrong. Or old project managers who don't like new fangled ways. Dom Mintoff was the Maltese prime minister at the time Malta gained independence from Britain in the 1960s. He was still a member of parliament in the early 1990s. His party, the Labour Party, had been in opposition for some time but won a general election in the mid 1990s, with a majority of one, and that one was Dom Mintoff. About 18 months after the general election he disagreed with something the prime minister was doing and so voted against the government. The prime minister had to resign and call a general election, and the Labour Party have never been in power again in Malta.

Develop a Communication Plan

We discuss that in the next section.

Monitoring Success

As the project progresses, monitoring the reactions of stakeholders is part of the control process. You need to maintain a relationship with the stakeholders so you can continually monitor their emotional responses and predict their reactions. Hopefully the stakeholders react as expected and the project is successful. If they don't react as expected you may need to go back and revisit your influence strategy.

Also, if things change, either internally or in the external environment, that may have an impact on the stakeholders and their perceptions. So you may also need your influence competence to keep them in line with your strategy or even change your influence tactics.

COMMUNICATING WITH STAKEHOLDERS

In the last chapter we saw that communication is a key competence for project leaders, especially on information systems and organizational change projects. It is through communication that the project manager builds relationships with the stakeholders. In this section we consider how to develop a communication strategy with the general stakeholders and in the next with a very specific and key stakeholder, the project sponsor.

There are several questions to be asked when developing a communication plan with stakeholders:

- Who are the target audience?
- What are the objectives of each communication?
- What information will be communicated by whom and when?
- How will feedback be encouraged?
- What media will be used?

Target audience. Through the stakeholder analysis we identified the target audience. You must just take care to understand the target audience and properly research the parent organization so you are aware of the power and influence networks within it. Also be aware that you must segment the market; not every stakeholder needs the same message, nor the same mode of delivering the message. The stakeholder register will tell you the key messages to be communicated to each stakeholder, and the best way of communicating with them.

Objectives of each communication. Plan each communication carefully and understand the objectives of each. Possible objectives may be:

- to raise people's awareness of the project;
- to gain their commitment to the project;
- to reduce their opposition;
- to keep other business areas informed;
- to promote key messages;
- to demonstrate commitment to the project's requirements;
- to make communication two way;
- to ensure all the stakeholders have a common understanding of the project;

- to maximize potential benefits from the project by gaining everyone's support.

We will return to the need to make communication two-way shortly.

Who and when? This addresses the appropriate use of power and authority to lead stakeholders. Not all the communication will be made by the project manager. Sometimes the sponsor needs to be involved, especially if communicating to the board, or other key senior stakeholders. The message will be more powerful if it comes from the sponsor, and other senior managers may be more willing to listen. That may also be necessary when talking to the boards of key customers or suppliers. He or she must convey a sense of achievement and motivation on behalf of the project manager in order to motivate the stakeholders and move the project forward. Sometimes the communication needs to be done by a technical expert, who will have more technical credibility with the stakeholders, but when using your empowerment competencies and nominating a technical expert for a talk remember to get them to talk in layman's terms, when talking to a non-technical audience.

Encourage feedback. It is important to encourage feedback. It is done through engaging communication, and contributes to critical analysis and judgement and through that to development. So that means at communication meetings you must:

- show people you are listening through your body language – don't stare out the window when they are asking a question, or cross your arms (which is seen as a barrier);
- answer their questions, and if you can't do not attempt to answer them straight away, ensure you do so later;
- when appropriate make changes to the project that show you are listening to their suggestions.

In making changes to the project you must not make changes that reduce the value of the project, so the increased cost must not be greater then the increased benefit. Somebody might have a really good idea that causes a large increase in benefit for a small increase in cost, or even an increase in benefit for a reduction in cost. Adopt the idea and give due credit, which shows your emotional resilience. But it can also be useful to make superficial changes, ones that cause a small increase in cost and a commensurate increase in benefit. They don't change the value of the project, but they show you are listening, a key component of communication. You have to avoid changes that increase cost for no increase in benefit, which should come from your critical analysis and judgement.

Media. Lead your audience by choosing your communication media in accordance with the severity of the message to be conveyed. Non-urgent scheduled communication, such as project meetings or monthly status reports, should be sent by mail or stored in the assigned server space. Those forms of communication use media that is mainly designed for one-way communication from you to the stakeholders. In case of plan deviations or other issues you should use media that allow for interaction with and timely provision of information to the stakeholders. This includes telephone or online media in case of urgent problems, and even face-to-face meetings or video conferencing in case of highly serious issues. The latter allows for the exchange of many communication cues, that is, not only the spoken word about the issues at stake, but also the body language and communication style, which has a major impact on the credibility of the message you send out to the stakeholders. Choosing the right media shows your sensitivity for the situation and your competence in managing resources, such as stakeholders. Moreover, it shows your self-awareness, which increases your credibility in crisis situations and supports your ability to influence. With external stakeholders you may want to communicate via television, newspapers or radio, or open days to make the communication two-way. With people in the parent organization but outside the project, newsletters and videos can help win their support and keep them informed of progress. Rodney has also known project managers who have held regular lunches with key stakeholders. For the project team, social networking sites can help build a sense of family.

Communication Plan

Table 5.3, overleaf, is an example of a communication plan for communicating with the stakeholders in Table 5.2.

COMMUNICATING WITH SPONSORS

Work done by Ralf Müller (Turner and Müller 2003) has shown that on high performing projects:

- the client and the project manager work together in partnership, working for the good of the project towards mutually beneficial objectives;
- the client imposes medium levels of structure on the project manager, giving guidance as to how he or she thinks the project should be done, but leaving the project manager flexibility to deal with unknown risks and other uncertainties.

These are two necessary conditions for project success. Unfortunately, they do not come automatically. Project managers must earn a certain level of trust before sponsors allow them enter into a partnership or provide them with sufficient

Table 5.3   Communication plan

Stakeholder	Objective of communication	Media
Board	Win finance for project	Board presentation
Marketing	Win and maintain sponsorship	Regular meetings
Operations	Gather user input Training in use of plant	Consultation meetings Briefing meetings
Local residents	Inform about cleanliness of plant and lack of traffic Inform about job opportunities	Advertisements in press Radio appearances Site open day
Local politicians	Inform about job opportunities Win support	Briefing meeting Continuing reports
Local media	Gain positive commitment	Communication via press office Open days
Environmental activists	Inform about cleanliness of plant and lack of traffic	Briefing meeting Continuing project reports
etc.		

freedom to manage their day-to-day business without much control. The sponsor is responsible for ensuring that the project is managed in the best interest of the sponsoring organization. What often happens is that the sponsor does not trust the project's manager, and lays down strict rules as to how the project is to be done. This undermines motivation and leads to work-to-rule behaviour on the part of project manager and team. Here each party tries to win at the other's advantage, with overall detrimental effect on the project. That is where the project leader needs to show emotional resilience. Overcoming the temptation to work just in accordance with the rules, and motivating himself or herself and others for the achievement of the (higher) project goals for the good of all stakeholders identifies the true leader, which then earns the credibility needed for entering into partnership with the sponsor and avoiding unnecessary control. But what is it that leads to the initial tension in the project manager-sponsor relationship?

The Principal–Agency Relationship

Part of the reason for this is that the client and project manager are in a principal–agent relationship, (Jensen 2000). Such a relationship exists where the principal (here the client or sponsor) relies upon an agent (here the project manager) to undertake a task on their behalf. There are two problems associated with such a relationship:

1. *The adverse selection problem.* Strictly this occurs at the point where the principal appoints the agent to perform the task. The principal cannot be certain they have appointed the best person, or even that they have appointed a competent person. But it leads the principal to be unsure why the agent is doing the things he or she is doing throughout the project. Hence the principal feels inclined to impose high structure to make sure things are done as the principal wants, and competently.

2. *The moral hazard problem.* Economic theory suggests that the rational human being will act rationally in any situation to maximize profit from the situation. Thus the project manager (agent) will be acting to maximize his or her profit from the project, and will only work to maximize the client's if their objectives happen to be aligned. The client should be aware of this and work hard through the contract to incentivize the project manager to achieve his or her objectives. Also the project manager will usually take a medium to long term view and will want to continue working for this client into the future, and so a good job on this project will lead to future projects. However, if this is a truly one-off relationship (as happens in the building industry where there are a large number of clients and contractors) then each may try to increase their profit at the other's expense (for example by project managers staying in expensive hotel rooms, flying business class, or renting expensive cars, and by sponsors coercing the project manager into unacceptable living and working conditions, or working times and locations). This ends in a so called win–lose game. But Ralf Müller's work shows that there is no such thing as a win–lose game on projects; it is either win-win or lose–lose. Projects are not a cake of fixed size. If you work together in partnership (win–win game) you can increase the size of the cake and both take home more. But if the client and contractor try to win at the other's expense, they reduce the size of the cake and both take home less. Both lose, just one more than the other; it is the lawyers who win ultimately. So the moral hazard problem causes the mistrust where the client thinks the project manager is trying to increase their profit at the client's expense.

Thus, we see the need to work in partnership and with a certain level of empowerment of the project manager to run the day-to-day business of the project. However, there are two management problems that get in the way (adverse selection and moral hazard), which can only be resolved through leadership behaviour, which we now discuss.

The Client's Comfort Needs

In order to minimize the mistrust that arises from this relationship, the project manager needs to lead the client in a way to keep them feeling comfortable in terms of the information and communication he or she receives. The client has several needs to feel comfortable with the performance on the project: He or she wants to know that:

1. the project's output is going to function to deliver the desired outcomes and benefit;
2. an appropriate process has been adopted to deliver the project's output in an optimum way;
3. the project will be completed within the performance targets of time, cost and quality;
4. the project manager is behaving in a trustworthy manager;
5. appropriate controls are in place to achieve all the above, including 4.

The project manager needs to communicate with the client in such a way to satisfy these needs. This is about understanding the client's emotional response to the principal–agent relationship, and the adverse selection and moral hazard problems, and communicating with them in a way that addresses the problems and ameliorates the client's concerns.

The Client's Communication Needs

Bob Graham (2007) suggests that in developing information systems you don't ask yourself what data you need but what questions you want answering. The questions the client wants answering are:

- *Questions of product and process*: will the end deliverable function to produce the output and has the right process been adopted to deliver it in an optimal way?
- *Questions of performance*: are sufficient resources being applied to deliver the project in the required timescale, but within the agreed budget?
- *Questions of surprise avoidance*: is the project manager taking the best decisions and behaving professionally and in the client's best interest?

Frequency and Medium of Communication

So how often should the project manager make reports to the client and in what form? The project manager should make regular written reports informing the client of progress. The timing of reports can be calendar-driven or event-driven. Calendar-driven means reports should be made at regular intervals and event-driven means they are made at major milestones. Calendar driven reports are essential; you should make written reports at regular intervals. Ralf Müller found that there was a tension between clients and project managers on this issue (Turner and Müller 2003). Clients wanted almost daily reports but project managers would like to make them once every two months. A balance needs to be struck between the need to keep the client feeling comfortable and the cost of the reports (which the client ultimately pays for). Making reports once every two weeks or once per month is a good balance. Ralf also found that where the client asks for the reports the project performs better and where they don't the project does not perform so well. This was another necessary condition for project success; the client should show interest and ask for the reports.

But clients can also be somewhat schizophrenic. They trust the written reports but they do not. They trust the written reports to give a true picture of project progress, but they don't trust the reports to give a true picture of risks and issues being faced by the project. For this they want to have face-to-face meetings with the project manager. At such meetings they can ask the project manager about risks and issues and read their body language to see if they are giving a true representation. But the client does not trust the quantitative data the project manager gives at the face-to-face meeting. So the client wants the written reports, once a month, for progress data, and the face-to-face meeting, once a week, for risks and issues. There is a balance between fact-based reporting and opinion-based reporting; each compliments the other, and they build trust. When trust is low, control is high, and vice versa. But how can we develop trust in order to lower the control from the sponsor?

DEVELOPING AND MAINTAINING TRUST

Trust is an important component of project leadership. When communicating with stakeholders, they have to trust that:

- you are competent and can deliver the project within its performance targets;
- the project business case is valid and based on sound data;
- you will behave professionally to maximize the client's benefits from the project;
- you are somebody they can work with.

Francis Hartman (2000) suggests a three-colour model for trust:

Blue trust – trust in competence. The first is trust that somebody is actually competent to do the task you have asked them to do. This is related to the adverse selection problem from the principal–agency relationship: is the agent competent to do the task they are doing on behalf of the principal, were they the best person for the job, and are they taking the best decisions on the project to maximize the performance of the project? This exists not just between the sponsor and the project manager, but between the project manager and the team members. The project manager is principal to the team members as agents. Francis Hartman suggests that blue trust grows slowly, it takes months for somebody to prove their competence. But it is also soundly based, and is also only lost slowly. If somebody makes a mistake, the trust in their competence can be dented, but then it can continue to grow again. It takes months of poor performance for it to be lost. Therefore blue trust is like a pyramid, growing slowly but only decaying slowly.

Yellow trust – trust in ethics. The second is trust that somebody will behave professionally and ethically. When the project manager says the business case is based on sound data it truly is, and he or she will work in the best interests of the client and not just in his or her own best interests. This is related to the moral hazard problem in the principal–agent relationship: it is the trust that the agent will work in the principal's interest and not just their own, and so the decisions the agent is taking will maximize the client's outcomes and not just their own. Oliver Williamson (1999), based on the economic idea that the rational person will act rationally to maximize their economic outcome from a situation thinks, there is no such things as yellow trust; it is a straight economic decision. If behaving professionally will lead to the best medium- to long-term outcomes people will behave professionally; but if there are only short-term outcomes people will tend to act to maximize their short-term outcomes. However, Rodney has spoken to project managers who say that they will always behave professionally, but Oliver Williamson might still say that is an economic decision because they are concerned about their reputation in the industry. Yellow trust grows over a period of days, but can be lost instantly. So it is like an upright, right-angled triangle. Rodney's experience is that it is like a mask. Somebody can appear trustworthy. But if the mask moves and you see the devil underneath, the other person can never refit the mask completely; you can always see the devil underneath.

Red trust – trust in the working relationship. The third trust is a belief that we can work with somebody. When we meet somebody, our personalities click or they don't. If project team members' personalities don't click, the project manager has to work on trying to overcome that problem. Francis Hartman suggests that red trust builds in micro-seconds on first meeting, and runs like a rolling wave. When Rodney worked for Coopers and Lybrand in the 1980s, he did one job that went so badly a TV documentary was made about it. (Coopers and Lybrand were not the lead consultants on the job and so were not blamed by the programme for the problems; indeed they were not mentioned at all.) The director on the job told Rodney afterwards the minute he walked into the client's office he decided he didn't like him. He said that a sufficient condition for a job going well was that he liked the client, and a necessary condition for a job going badly was he didn't like the client. So if he liked the client the job was guaranteed to go well and in all jobs that went badly he hadn't clicked with the client. There were some jobs that went well where he didn't like the client. So if you have red trust, the project will go well.

Francis Hartman also identifies three mixed colours of trust. In all relationships all three types of trust are important, but in certain contexts two are more important than the third.

Green trust – business trust. In a business context trust in competence and ethics are particularly important. This is why professionalism is so important to project managers. Certification is a badge of competence and membership of a professional association with a code of ethics, such as the Association for Project Management (APM) or the Project Management Institute (PMI) is a badge of professional behaviour. The client in appointing the agent has increased confidence that they can be less concerned by the adverse selection and moral hazard problems.

Purple trust – sporting trust. In a sporting context, trust in competence and the personal relationship is very important. Several years ago Rodney was watching Manchester United play. At one point Ruud van Nistleroy and David Beckham were in the box. Ruud van Nistleroy had the ball, but the goalie was between him and the ball. But David Beckham was unmarked with the open goal mouth in front of him. So Ruud van Nistleroy passed David Beckham the ball and David Beckham scored the goal. Ruud van Nistleroy passed David Beckham the ball because he trusted his competence to score the goal. About five minutes later David Beckham was tripped up in the box and Manchester United were awarded a penalty. Under normal circumstances when a good goal scorer like David Beckham is tripped he would take the penalty. But Ruud van Nistleroy took the penalty. David Beckham trusted Ruud van Nistleroy's competence to score the penalty, but also they swapped goals. Since Ruud van Nistleroy had let David Beckham score his goal, David Beckham let Ruud van Nistleroy score his goal. There was the social trust as well. Project team members need to trust that each other is competent and that they will give each other due recognition for their contributions to the project.

Orange trust – family trust. In a family context the social and relationship trust are particularly important.

Francis Hartman also suggests how the three different types of trust affect the working relationships on project teams against six success factors (see Table 5.4). The project leader needs to be aware how these six factors affect the working relationship of the project team members, including his or her relationship with the team and work at making sure they all work.

Table 5.4 suggests we should be inclusive. Project managers are good at that. Rodney was at the IPMA World Congress one year, and was talking to a delegate who said it was his first time at the conference. The delegate said it was great because people were going out of their way to talk to him and make him feel part of the team, whereas at other conferences it was very difficult to break into existing cliques. That is Rodney's experience at the Academy of Management in the US; you seem to be constantly looking at people's backs as they stand in tight circles. Work hard at making new people feel welcome in the project team.

Table 5.4   Trust and the working relationships on project teams

Success factor	Blue – Competence	Yellow – Ethics	Red – Social
Communication	Understand common ground	Respect confidence, avoid rumour	Nobody is irrational, understand world views
Ownership	Respect expertise and contributions	Accept weaknesses, offer support	Work well with experts, accept their views
Risk	Understand risk in the team context	Be open	Treat everyone as equals
Creativity	Allow team member to be creative	Acknowledge contributions	Don't let emotion colour your judgement
Fun	Recognize contributions	Have fun with people not about people	Work hard at this in crises
Tribalism	Define primary and support roles	Be inclusive	Manage conflict objectively

AVOIDING AND RESOLVING CONFLICT

Table 5.4 suggests that in order to maintain the social trust in the project team, especially to maintain the sense of the team as a team, we need to resolve conflict objectively and so we now consider how to do that. Conflict can arise either because of issues in the working relationships of the project team, or because of things that the project manager, project sponsor or other senior managers do. Issues in the project team can arise because people have different perceptions of the project's goals. That's not just individual project milestones, but the definition of the project output, the desired outcomes or even the long term impact. Project team members can also disagree about the best method of achieving the project goals, the technology to be used, or how work should be divided between the different functions. Conflict can of course arise from people's emotional response to changes on the project. People can feel frustrated that they did not achieve their objectives, and then blame other people and so feel anger. There can also be issues between different functional departments, or between functional departments and the project. Different departmental goals can lead to conflict, or long-standing departmental grudges; or just stereotyping. Bob Graham (2007) relates a story of a project he worked on where the engineers were blaming the marketing department for selling something impossible to make, and the marketing department were blaming the engineers for deliberately sabotaging the system. Bob had to work hard on resolving the problem by getting them both to appreciate the other's viewpoint. Finally there can be different cultural perspectives which can lead to different perceptions and hence to conflict. Even the conflict between the marketers and the engineers just discussed was partially due to their different cultures as well as the stereotyping of each other.

Things managers do that cause conflict mainly arise through a failure to communicate properly with the stakeholders, and by communicate we mean consult as well as transmit. People may not properly understand the benefit from the project, and therefore why the change is needed. They may feel that recently they have been subjected to too much change and so resist just through feeling overloaded. People may feel that managers have not sought feedback, or the feedback given has just been ignored. That is why it is important for leaders to show they are listening, through their body language, by answering questions, and by making some changes to the project in response to the concerns of the stakeholders. Finally you want people to fully internalize the change. Arthur Schopenhauer said every new idea goes through three stages:

- first people think it is stupid;
- then they think it is dangerous;
- then they think they believed that all along.

As a manager you have to lead people through the three stages; do not expect them to go in one step to accepting and internalizing the proposed change. First people need persuading that the proposed change is feasible and it will provide benefit. Then they will recognize problems in the change, how it will change their working environment, and so they will resist the idea. You need to persuade them that it will work, and it will be beneficial to the organization and they will be better off with the change than without it. Then you can get them to internalize the change and accept that it is a good idea they are committed to. But you must manage people through that process and not expect them to go to internalizing the change in one leap.

It is best to avoid having conflict occur, by recognizing possible sources and defusing them before they lead to conflict. But if conflict occurs there are three possible ways of defusing it:

Avoidance. This sounds fairly cowardly but that is not what is meant. Sometimes the conflicting parties don't need to work together on the project. They can both do their work without impacting on the other. So they can be simply asked to work in separate rooms. In that way the conflict is avoided.

Confrontation. This also sounds negative. Sometimes the conflict needs to be addressed head on – it is confronting the conflict, not the conflicting parties. Hold workshops to try to properly identify the problem that is leading to the conflict and solving the problem. The way Rodney Turner (2009) describes project start-up workshops is effectively confronting a conflict before it occurs. Project start-up workshops are conducted to avoid the storm phase of team formation. When a team first assembles, there can be differences of opinion about the project's objectives, plans and responsibilities, and you hold a start-up workshop to resolve those issues before they lead to conflict. Rodney worked once with a consultant who ran conflict resolution workshops. He described a workshop he held once where a contractor had made a silly claim, and so the client panicked and asked for such a workshop. In one day the issue was identified and solved and the client and contractor parted as friends. But at the end of the meeting the client asked the contractor why they had made such a silly claim; surely they knew it was silly. The contractor said yes it was a silly claim, but they had been trying for months to get the client to address the issue without success, so the only way of getting them to sit up and take notice was making a silly claim.

Diffusion. Through diffusion you try to dilute the conflict. You try to spread it around. Make the conflicting parties part of a larger team where their conflict becomes less significant. Or try to change the definition of the project so the disagreement about the goals or work methods is less significant. So instead of separating the conflicting parties you just try to make them part of a larger group where their disagreement is less significant. But it can backfire if they poison the working relationships of other people.

Developing an influence strategy for the project by performing the stakeholder assessment as suggested above, and then developing a communication plan can help to identify and avoid some of the sources of conflict. Also seeking top management support and having senior managers show commitment to the project can support the project.

SUMMARY

In this chapter we have looked at how the emotionally competent project leaders can build relationships with the project team and project stakeholders. The inspiring project leader needs to motivate the project team and stakeholders to support the project, and can do that by communicating well with them. Communication is often something project managers are not comfortable with as suggested in Chapter 4, but it is a significant element of project leadership. The project manager needs to show sensitivity to build trust, and identify and resolve conflict. Throughout the project the leader needs to show emotional intelligence. They need to be aware of their own response to trust, emotions and conflict, and be aware of their own commitment to the project and communicate that to stakeholders. Once aware of their own responses they need to manage those responses and be aware of the responses of others. They can then manage their relationships with others, manage the relationships between others and manage the relationship of others to the project.

CHAPTER 6

TOWARDS A LEADERSHIP COMPETENCE THEORY OF PROJECT PERFORMANCE

In this chapter we integrate the subjects addressed in the earlier chapters into an emerging theory of project performance, based on the leadership competencies of the project manager. We finish the chapter with a brief look into the future of leadership in projects.

LEADERSHIP COMPETENCE AS A PROJECT SUCCESS FACTOR

Throughout this book, and particularly in Chapter 4, we have shown that leadership competencies are a factor for project success. To be a success factor, different combinations of competencies are needed for different types of projects. Table 6.1 summarizes this by showing the main competencies related to project success in different types of projects. However, as important as the main competencies are for project success, they do not act in a vacuum and they need to be complemented by further competencies which only become important in specific circumstances. Their importance is dependent on the specifics of an individual project within a project type, such as contract type, complexity and so on (see Tables 4.2 to 4.4). Supporting dimensions of competence are not directly related to project success. They complement the other competencies for a well-rounded personality of the project manager.

Successful leadership is dependent on finding the right leadership style for the people to be led. People are different in different project types, and so are the required leadership styles. Looking at Table 6.1 from left to right we see a continuum from tangible to intangible outputs of projects. The most tangible are the outputs from engineering and construction projects. This is followed by slightly more intangible outputs in IT projects, which are typically a combination of systems (hardware and software) and work processes. Finally organizational change projects create the most intangible outputs, as they are about processes and working relationships.

At the extremes of the continuum from tangible to intangible project outputs, the projects with tangible outputs require project managers who know what is expected in their role and 'just do it', with attention to detail and commitment, and without a

Table 6.1   Hierarchy of importance of leadership competencies by project type

	Project type		
	Engineering and Construction	**IT**	**Organizational Change**
Main competencies	Conscientiousness Sensitivity (Vision)	Communication Self-awareness Developing others (Vision)	Communication Motivation (Vision)
Situational competencies	Managing resources, empowering, critical analysis and judgement, strategic perspective, emotional resilience, influence, conscientiousness		
Supporting competencies	Achieving, intuitiveness		

far reaching vision. They sense what is going on in the team through empathy and interpersonal sensitivity and lead the team by example, offering themselves as a role model in terms of what they say and do.

Projects with intangible outcomes require an active, energetic and charismatic or transformational leader. These managers typically score high on vision, but should be careful in using too much of this competence. Too much vision can be a distraction from planned daily achievements. However, their accessible way of communicating with team members and engaging them by actively linking their personal objectives with those of the project makes these project managers best suitable for these projects.

Projects in the middle of the continuum require leaders who can balance the extremes. These leaders must be outgoing, accessible and engaging in their communication, but also stimulate individual team members' willingness to perform through individual incentives, such as personal development, often in the form of learning about latest technologies or methods. Dealing with the extroverted requirements for a good communicator and the introverted desires of the team members, in the context of ever changing requirements in dynamic industries such as IT, requires a good control of their own feelings, thus a lot of self-awareness and ability to manage their own feelings.

A LEADERSHIP COMPETENCE THEORY OF PROJECT PERFORMANCE

Figure 6.1 shows our theory for reaching project performance through appropriate leadership.

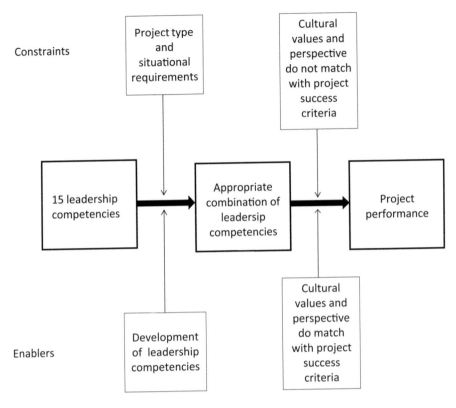

Figure 6.1   **Leadership competence based theory of project performance**

The central component is the appropriate combination of the 15 leadership dimensions for a given project. An appropriate combination leads to optimal project performance.

The combination of the 15 dimensions into the appropriate set for effective leadership within the context of a given project is enabled through the leadership development and practice. This may involve training, experience, mentoring and so on. However, the best mix of leadership dimensions is situational and depends on the project type and the various peculiarities of a project (such as contract type, complexity, and so on).

Therefore, leadership competencies must be developed before we can use them, but the project type plus the situational circumstances of the project limit the choices of combinations of leadership dimensions that are successful in a given project. A successful project manager must therefore have a larger pool of competences than is required at any one time, of which he or she selects and combines those that are the right ones for his or her current project.

The outcome of the right combination of leadership styles, appropriately applied, is project performance. This performance, however, is a matter of perception. The perception of good performance is enabled through a match between the cultural values (such as importance of customer satisfaction, Chapter 4) and the perspective of the individual (such as the sponsor or user) towards the project. A mismatch can hinder the recognition of good performance. All of which supports the need to agree the success criteria and their measurement upfront (which we said is a necessary condition for project success).

There are a number of assumptions underlying this model. These include whether the organization is able to identify the project managers' leadership profiles, the types of project the organization runs, and the existence of a target profile for a given type of project. However, we suggested that an organization should have a career structure for project managers, with defined competences at different levels to manage the types of projects it undertakes. Furthermore it assumes the existence of clearly defined success criteria and an understanding of how their values are interpreted in a given culture. This must be developed before the model can be used in practice.

The model reflects current understanding of the link between leadership and project performance. This understanding will, of course, further develop in the years to come.

THE WAY FORWARD

In this book we have challenged the two beliefs that project management is only about tools and techniques and can be applied universally by all project managers to all types of project. We showed that project managers and their leadership style are a critical success factor in projects. We identified an under-representation of leadership literature in project management and provided a summary of the leadership theories of the past 80 years. Then we looked into recent research and identified the particular leadership competences needed in different project types. Finally we developed a hierarchy of importance of competencies and a process theory for the application of these competencies.

What will the future bring us? Since 2006 we have seen a steady increase in research studies on leadership on projects, mainly from an emotional intelligence perspective. PMI has recently funded further research in this area, and project management researchers are joining the professional interest groups in emotional intelligence research, such as the Consortium for Research in Emotional Intelligence in Organizations, which is founded by Daniel Goleman and based in the Graduate School of Applied and Professional Psychology at Rutgers University. This group seeks to catalyze research on best practices for developing emotional competence, and the impact of emotional intelligence in leadership and organizations. The coming years will allow an understanding of leadership and the associated competencies at a more detailed level. This may be, for example, through the growing awareness of the functioning of the brain, which led recently to the identification of mirror-neurons. These neurons impact our social behaviour and the results of the research offer a partial explanation to many as yet misunderstood phenomena in human behaviour and their impact on leadership.

Training and development of leadership styles will become more productive and more diversified in organizations that take national cultural differences and organizational governance practices into account. A sensitive approach of this kind will provide for better economic and socially acceptable use of world resources. In this book we have shown how leadership can contribute to this aim.

REFERENCES

Bar-on, R. (2006), 'The bar-on model of emotional-social intelligence (ESI)', *Psicothema Revista de Psicologia*, 18: suppl., pp. 13–25.

Barnard, C.I. (1938), *The Functions of the Executive* (Cambridge, MA: Harvard University Press).

Barnard, J. (1999), 'The empowerment of problem-solving teams: Is it an effective management tool?', *Journal of Applied Management Studies* 8:1, pp. 73–84.

Bass, B.M. (1990), 'From transactional to transformational leadership: Learning to share the vision', *Organisational Dynamics* 18:3, pp. 19–31.

Belbin, R.M. (1986), *Management Teams* (London: Heinemann).

Bennis, W., and Nanus, B. (1985), *Leaders: The Strategies for Taking Charge* (New York: Harper and Row).

Blake, R.R. and Mouton, S.J. (1978), *The New Managerial Grid* (Houston, TX: Gulf).

Boyatzis, R.E. (1982), *The Competent Manager: A Model for Effective Performance* (New York, NY: Wiley).

Boyatzis, R., Goleman, D. and Rhee, K.S. (2000), 'Clustering Competence in Emotional Intelligence', in *Handbook of Emotional Intelligence* R. Bar-on and J.D.A. Parker (eds), (San Francisco: Jossey-Bass), pp. 343–362.

Bredin, K., and Söderlund, J. (2006), 'HRM and project intensification in R&D companies: A study of Volvo Car Corporation and AstraZeneca', *R&D Management* 36:5, pp. 467–485.

Briggs-Myers, I. (1992), *Gifts Differing* (Palo-Alto: Consulting Psychologists Press).

Burns, T., and Stalker, G.M. (1994), *The Management of Innovation* (New York: Oxford University Press).

Cattell, R.B., Eber, H.W. and Tatsuoka, M.M. (1970), *Handbook for the 16PF* (Illinois: IPAT).

Clarke, R.N. and Howell, R. (2009), *Emotional Intelligence and Projects: A pilot research project investigating relationships between EI abilities, project manager competences, and transformational leadership behaviors, and the impact of EI training amongst UK project managers* (Newtown Square, USA: Project Management Institute).

Collins, J.C., and Porras, J.I. (1991), 'Organizational vision and visionary organizations', *California Management Review*, 34:Fall, pp. 30–52.

Collinson, D., Plan, K., and Wilkinson, R. (2000), *Fifty Eastern Thinkers* (London: Routledge).

Crawford, L.H. (2005), 'Senior management perceptions of project management competence', *International Journal of Project Management.* 23:1, pp. 7–16.

Crawford, L.H. (2007), 'Developing Individual Competence', in *The Gower Handbook of Project Management*, 4th edition, J.R. Turner (ed), (Gower, Aldershot, UK), pp. 677–694 .

Crawford, L., Hobbs, B., and Turner, J.R. (2005), *Project Categorization Systems* (Newtown Square, PA: Project Management Institute).

Dainty, A.R.J., Cjeng, M. and Moore, D.R. (2005), 'Competency-based model for predicting construction project managers' performance', *Journal of Management in Engineering*, January, pp. 2–9.

D'Herbemont, O., Cesar, B., Etcheber, P and Curtin, T. (1998), *Managing Sensitive Projects: Lateral Approach*, revised edition (London: Plagrave Macmillan).

Dolfi, J. and Andrews, E.J. (2007), 'The subliminal characteristics of project managers: An exploratory study of optimism overcoming challenges in the project management work environment', *International Journal of Project Management* 25:7, pp. 674–682.

Dreyfus, C. (2008), 'Identifying competencies that predict effectiveness of R&D managers', *Journal of Management Development* 27:1, pp. 76–91.

Dulewicz, V., and Higgs, M. (2000), 'Emotional intelligence: A review and evaluation study', *Journal of Managerial Psychology* 15:4, pp. 341–368.

Dulewicz, V., and Higgs, M. (2003), 'Leadership at the top: The need for emotional intelligence in organizations', *International Journal of Organizational Analysis* 11:3, pp. 194–210.

Dulewicz, V., and Higgs, M. (2004), 'Can emotional intelligence be developed?', *International Journal of Human Resource Management* 15:1, pp. 95–111.

Dulewicz, V., and Higgs, M. (2005), 'Assessing leadership styles and organizational context', *Journal of Managerial Psychology* 20:1, pp. 105–123.

Ekman, P., (2004), *Emotions Revealed: Understanding Faces and Feelings*, new edition (London: Phoenix).

Elkins, T., and Keller, R.T. (2003), 'Leadership in research and development organizations: A literature review and conceptual framework', *The Leadership Quarterly* 14, pp. 587–606.

Fiedler, F.E., and Garcia, J.E. (1987), *New Approaches to Effective Leadership: Cognitive Resources and Organizational Performance* (New York: Wiley).

Frame, J.D. (2003), *Managing Projects in Organizations, How to Make the Best Use of Time, Techniques and People*, 3rd edition (San Francisco: Jossey-Bass).

Ghosh, A., and Chakraborty, S. (2007), 'Emotional intelligence: The next step in knowledge process outsourcing', *VISION – The Journal of Business Perspective* 12:1, pp. 19–30.

Gardner, L., and Stough, C. (2002), 'Examining the relationship between leadership and emotional intelligence in senior level managers', *Leadership & Organization Development Journal* 23:2, pp. 68–78.

Goleman, D. (1995), *Emotional Intelligence* (New York, NY: Bantam Books).

Goleman, D. (2001), 'An EI-Based Theory of Performance', in *The Emotionally Intelligent Workplace*, G. Cherniss and D. Goleman (eds), (San Francisco: Jossey-Bass).

Goleman, D. (2006), *Social Intelligence: The New Science of Human Relationships* (London, UK: Hutchinson).

Goleman, D., Boyatzis, R., and McKee, A. (2002), *Primal Leadership: Learning to Lead with Emotional Intelligence* (Boston, MA, USA: Harvard Business School Press).

Graham, R.G. (2007), 'Managing Conflict, Persuasion and Negotiation', in *The Gower Handbook of Project Management*, 4th edition, J.R. Turner (ed.), (Aldershot, UK: Gower), pp. 801–816.

Habermas, J. (1987), *Theorie des Kommunikativen Handelns* (Frankfurt am Main, Germany: Suhrkamp Verlag).

Hersey, P., and Blanchard, K.H. (1988), *Management of Organizational Behavior* (Englewood Cliffs, NJ: Prentice Hall).

Herzberg, F. (1987), 'One more time: How do you motivate employees?', *Harvard Business Review* 65:5, pp. 5–16.

Higgs, M. (2004), 'A study of the relationship between emotional intelligence and performance in UK call centres', *Journal of Managerial Psychology* 19:4, pp. 442–454.

House, R.J. (1971), 'A path-goal theory of leader effectiveness', *Administrative Science Quarterly* 16:3, pp. 321–338.

Huemann, M., Keegan, A., and Turner, J.R. (2007), 'Human resource management in the project-oriented company: A review', *International Journal of Project Management* 25:3, pp. 315–323.

Jensen, M.C. (2000), *A Theory of the Firm: Governance, Residual Claims and Organizational Forms*, new edition (Boston: Harvard University Press).

Judge, T.A., Colbert, A.E., and Ilies, R. (2004a), 'Intelligence and leadership: A quantitative review and test of theoretical propositions', *Journal of Applied Psychology* 89:3, pp. 542–552.

Judge, T.A., Piccolo, R.F. and Ilies, R. (2004b), 'The forgotten ones? The validity of consideration and initiating structure in leadership research', *Journal of Applied Psychology*, 89(1), 36.51.

Jugdev, K., Müller, R., and Hutchison, M. (2009), 'The Likely Interdependence of Strategic Management and Project Management Circa 2025', in *Project Management Circa 2025*, D.L. Cleland and B. Bidanda (eds), (Newtown Square, PA: Project Management Institute).

Keegan, A.E. and Den Hartog, D.N. (2004), 'Transformational leadership in a project-based environment: a comparative study of the leadership styles of project managers and line managers', *International Journal of Project Management* 22:8, pp. 609–618.

Kirkman, B.L., Rosen, B., Tesluk, P.E., and Gibson, C.B. (2004), 'The impact of team empowerment on virtual team performance: The moderating role of face-to-face interaction', *Academy of Management Journal* 47:2, pp. 175–192.

Kirkpatrick, S.A. and Locke, E.A. (1991), 'Leadership traits do matter', *Academy of Management Executive* 5:2, pp. 44–60.

KPMG (2005), *Global IT Project Management Survey* (USA: KPMG).

Labianca, G., Gray, B., and Brass, D.J. (2000), 'A grounded model of organizational schema change during empowerment', *Organization Science* 11:2, pp. 235–257.

Lee, C.H., and Bruvold, N.T. (2003), 'Creating value for employees: Investment in employee development', *International Journal of Human Resource Management* 14:6, pp. 981–1000.

Lee-Kelley, L. and Leong, K.L. (2003), 'Turner's five functions of project-based management and situational leadership in IT services projects', *International Journal of Project Management* 21:8, pp. 583–591.

Mahaney, R.C., and Lederer, A.L. (2006), 'The effect of intrinsic and extrinsic rewards for developers on information systems project success', *Project Management Journal* 37:4, pp. 42–54.

Margerison, M. and McCann, D. (1990), *Team Management: Practical New Approaches*, (London: Mercury Press).

Maslow, A. (1943), 'Preface to motivation theory', *Psychosomatic Medicine* 5:1, pp. 85–92.

Mayer, J.D. (1995), 'A framework for the classification of personality components', *Journal of Personality* 63:4, pp. 819–878.

Mayer, J.D., Roberts, R.D., and Barsade, J.D. (2008), 'Human abilities: emotional intelligence', in *Annual Review of Psychology*, Annual Reviews, 59, pp. 507–536.

Mayer, J.D. and Salovey, P. (1997), 'What is Emotional Intelligence', in *Emotional Development and Emotional Intelligence: Educational Implications*, P. Salovey and P. Sluyter (eds), (New York: Basic Books).

Mayer, J.D., Salovey, P., and Caruso, D.R. (2000), 'Emotional Intelligence as Zeitgeist, as Personality, and as Mental Ability', in *The Handbook of Emotional Intelligence*, R. Bar-on and D.A. Parker (eds), (San Francisco: Jossey-Bass), pp. 92–117.

Mayer, J.D., and Stevens, A.A. (1994), 'An emerging understanding of the reflective (meta-) experience of mood', *Journal of Research in Personality* 28:3, pp. 351–373.

McClelland, D.C. (1973), 'Testing for competence rather than for "intelligence"', *American Psychologist* 28:1, pp. 1–14.

McCrae, R.R., and John, O.P. (1992), 'An introduction to the five factor model and its application', *Journal of Personality* 60:2, pp. 175–215.

Mersino, A. (2007), *Emotional Intelligence for Project Managers* (New York: AMACOM).

Mordaunt, J., and Cornforth, C. (2004), 'The role of boards in the failure and turnaround of non-profit organizations', *Public Money & Management* 24:4, pp. 227–234.

Müller, R., and Turner, J.R. (2006), 'Leadership Competences and Their Successful Application in Different Types of Projects', in *Proceedings of IRNOP VII*, L. Ou and J.R. Turner (eds), October, pp. 212–223.

Müller, R., and Turner, J.R. (2007a), 'Matching the project manager's leadership style to project type', *International Journal of Project Management*, 25:1, pp. 21–32.

Müller, R., and Turner, J.R. (2007b), 'The influence of project managers on project success criteria and project success by type of project', *European Management Journal* 25:4, pp. 289–309.

Nonanka, I. and Takeuchi, H. (1995), *The Knowledge Creating Company* (Oxford University Press, Oxford, UK).

Parry, K. (2004), *The Seven Sins and the Seven Virtues of Leadership: Which Path Do We Follow?* CLME Leading Matters Symposium, 17 August 2005, Griffith University EcoCentre, Nathan, Australia. To be downloaded from http://www.griffith.edu.au/__data/assets/pdf_file/0006/40929/report-parry-leadership.pdf. Last access 2009–06–18.

Pease, A., and Pease, B. (2005), *The Definitive Book of Body Language* (London: Orion Books).

Pinto, J.K. and Slevin, D.P. (1988), 'Critical Success Factors in Effective Project Implementation', in *Project Management Handbook*, 2nd edition, D.I. Cleland and W.R. King (eds), (New York, NY: Van Nostrand Reinhold).

Project Management Institute (2007), *Construction Extension to the PMBOK Guide*, 3rd edition (Newtown Square, PA: Project Management Institute).

Porthouse, M., and Dulewicz, V. (2007), 'Agile Project Managers' Leadership Competencies', *Henley Management College Working Paper Series HWP 0714*, (Henley-on-Thames, UK: Henley Management College).

Saarni, C. (2000), 'Emotional Competence: A Developmental Perspective', in *Handbook of Emotional Intelligence*, R. Bar-on and J.D.A. Parker (eds), (San Francisco: Jossey-Bass).

Tannenbaum, R. and Schmidt, W.H. (1958), 'How to choose a leadership pattern', *Harvard Business Review* 36:2, pp. 95–101.

The Standish Group (1998), 'CHAOS '98: A Summary Review', *Standish Group Research Note*, pp. 1–4.

Thomas, J., Delisle, C., and Jugdev, K. (2002), *Selling Project Management to Senior Executives* (Newtown Square: Project Management Institute, Inc.).

Topping, K., Bremner, W., and Holmes, E.A. (2000), 'Social Competence: The Social Construction of the Concept', in *The Handbook of Emotional Intelligence*, R. Bar-on and J.D.A. Parker (eds), (San Francisco: Jossey-Bass), pp. 28–39.

Turner, J.R. (2007), *The Gower Handbook of Project Management*, 4th edition (Aldershot: Gower).

Turner, J.R., (2009), *The Handbook of Project Based Management*, 3rd edition (New York: McGraw-Hill)

Turner, J.R., Huemann, M., and Keegan, A.E., (2008), *Human Resource Management in the Project-Oriented Organization* (Newtown Square, PA: Project Management Institute).

Turner, J.R., Keegan, A.E. and Crawford, L.H. (2003), 'Delivering improved project management maturity through experiential learning', in *People in Project Management*, J.R. Turner (ed.), (Aldershot: Gower).

Turner, J.R. and Müller, R. (2004), 'Communication and cooperation on projects between the project owner as principal and the project manager as agent', *European Management Journal* 22:3, pp. 327–336.

Turner, J.R. and Müller, R. (2005), 'The Project Manager's Leadership Style as a Success Factor on Projects: A Literature Review', *Project Management Journal* 36:2, pp. 49–61.

Turner, J.R., and Müller, R. (2006), *Choosing Appropriate Project Managers: Matching Their Leadership Style to the Type of Project* (Newtown Square, PA: Project Management Institute).

Turner, J.R., Müller, R., and Dulewicz, V. (2009), 'Comparing the leadership styles of functional and project managers', *International Journal of Managing Projects in Business* 2:2, pp. 198–216.

Williamson, J.E., Pemberton, A.E., and Lounsbury, J.W. (2005), 'An investigation of career and job satisfaction in relation to personality traits of information professionals', *Library Quarterly* 75:2, pp. 122–141.

Williamson, O.E. (1999), *The Mechanisms of Governance*, new edition (New York: Oxford University Press).

Witt, L.A., Burke, L.A., Barrick, M.R., and Mount, M.K. (2002), 'The interactive effects of conscientiousness and agreeableness on job performance', *Journal of Applied Psychology* 87:1, pp. 164–169.

WordNet (2009), Online Dictionary, Cognitive Science Laboratory, Princeton University, USA. http://wordnetweb.princeton.edu/perl/webwn?s=personality. Last access: 2009–06–10.

INDEX

ADVANCES IN PROJECT MANAGEMENT and FUNDAMENTALS OF PROJECT MANAGEMENT SERIES

Project management has become a key competence for most organisations in the public and private sectors. Driven by recent business trends such as fewer management layers, greater flexibility, increasing geographical distribution and more project-based work, project management has grown beyond its roots in the construction, engineering and aerospace industries to transform the service, financial, computer, and general management sectors. In fact, a Fortune article rated project management as the number one career choice at the beginning of the 21st century.

Yet many organisations have struggled in applying the traditional models of project management to their new projects in the global environment. Project management offers a framework to help organisations to transform their mainstream operations and service performance. It is viewed as a way of organising for the future. Moreover, in an increasingly busy, stressful, and uncertain world it has become necessary to manage several projects successfully at the same time. According to some estimates the world annually spends well over $10 trillion (US) on projects. In the UK alone, more than £250 billion is spent on projects every year. Up to half of these projects fail! A major ingredient in the build-up leading to failure is often cited as the lack of adequate project management knowledge and experience.

Some organizations have responded to this situation by trying to improve the understanding and capability of their managers and employees who are introduced to projects, as well as their experienced project managers in an attempt to enhance their competence and capability in this area.

ADVANCES IN PROJECT MANAGEMENT

Advances in Project Management provides short, state of play, guides to the main aspects of the new emerging applications of project management including: maturity models, agile projects, extreme projects, six sigma and projects, human factors and leadership in projects, project governance, value management, virtual teams, project benefits.

Visit www.gowerpublishing.com/advancesinprojectmanagement for more information and a list of titles.